APPROPRIATE

ALSO BY PAISLEY REKDAL

POETRY

Nightingale

Imaginary Vessels

Animal Eye

The Invention of the Kaleidoscope

Six Girls Without Pants

A Crash of Rhinos

PROSE

*The Broken Country: On Trauma, a Crime,
and the Continuing Legacy of Vietnam*

Intimate: An American Family Photo Album

*The Night My Mother Met Bruce Lee:
Observations on Not Fitting In*

APPROPRIATE

A Provocation

Paisley Rekdal

W. W. NORTON & COMPANY
Independent Publishers Since 1923

For information about special discounts for bulk purchases, please contact
W. W. Norton Special Sales at specialsales@wwnorton.com or 800-233-4830

Manufacturing by LSC Communications, Harrisonburg
Production manager: Lauren Abbate

ISBN 978-1-324-00358-8 (pbk.)

W. W. Norton & Company, Inc., 500 Fifth Avenue, New York, N.Y. 10110
www.wwnorton.com

W. W. Norton & Company Ltd., 15 Carlisle Street, London W1D 3BS

1 2 3 4 5 6 7 8 9 0.

For my father,
who opened my mind to a world of books

Contents

APPROPRIATE

LETTER ONE

An Invitation

Dear X:

You asked at the end of last class whether I had an essay I might share with you about cultural appropriation. You asked because of the tense note on which our workshop ended the discussion of your poem, a monologue in the voice of a Black nurse who worked in your White grandmother's home in Georgia. Your poem was meant to be a complex double portrait of both the Black caregiver and your White grandmother, and the racist logic and history that bound them both. Did you, a young White person, the child of people you freely admitted had been shaped by racist beliefs, have any claim or relationship to this voice? Our workshop worried this question for an hour without resolving it. And while our discussion never devolved, as I was concerned it might, into open hostility, it also didn't make anyone feel better for having participated in it, nor did it settle the questions your poem raised to anyone's satisfaction. You still wanted, you said, an answer. Frankly, so do I.

I could tell by your subdued demeanor when you approached me that you were afraid your poem had caused pain, and that there might be some future, perhaps public, fallout for it. Perhaps there will be. I assume there won't, because your classmates took the poem and you with pretty good humor, respect, and patience, even when they disagreed—sometimes vehemently—with the poem itself. All of us acknowledged that authorial intentions don't finally matter to how we read a creative work that fails, but what does it mean for a poem like yours to fail, exactly? And what are the implications if we said your poem had succeeded? When we write in the voice of people unlike ourselves, what do we risk besides the possibility of getting certain facts, histories, and perspectives wrong? And was your poem, to certain audiences, perhaps always meant, if not to fail, then to be seen as an ethical lapse?

You should know how many other students I've taught over the years whose work has raised the same questions, X. You should know, too, how much I respect the ways you took your classmates' criticism during our discussion. You didn't lash out or sulk, you didn't try to justify or explain anything away. You sat and listened, perhaps the hardest thing to do when a group of strangers ponders whether your words and images, and by implication you, are inherently racist. Your desire to "get it right," as you expressed yesterday afternoon, was everywhere evident in your response to your classmates' concerns, and it requires that I now find the right essay to address your question around the ethics of creative expression. While I have a number of articles and books I recommend reading, I can't think of one that speaks to a young writer trying to probe the limitations of her imagination, one who is both open-minded about the question of appropriation and also, reasonably, terrified. I know when you and other students ask me for such an essay, you are asking if I can find the single argument that would either rationalize or dismiss the practice; you are asking me to tell you how cultural appropriation is generally defined, why and if writers think it's always wrong, whether it's been done well before in literature and how. This is an essay I imagine the other students in our class would want to read after our conversation; it's an essay that I, as a writer, have never found.

Like many writers today, I believe writing in the voice of someone outside my subject position surely crosses a line, but which one, exactly? Writing is mastered over the course of a life, and perhaps you suspect the truth of mastery, which is that it's achieved by both practicing *and* unlearning the lessons teachers like me drill into you at school, lessons that, while they lay the groundwork for producing good stories and poems, prove insufficient for creating our greatest work, which often disrupts the messages we've been taught. As writers, we absorb much of our technique through reading, more so than through class discussion, and yet books, too, fall short when it comes to determining just what is the *right* kind of appropriation to attempt, since so much of writing is appropriative, and so much of appropriative writing is historically contextualized. Here is where the workshop might have stepped in with good advice, but as you yourself have seen, people would rather gnaw off the fingers of their right hand than talk through the tangled arguments around cultural appropriation.

Because what we're really talking about with cultural appropriation, X, is identity, and while we all have identities, few of us are prepared to unravel the Gordian knot of social realities, history, and fantasy that constitute a self and its attendant ideas of race, ethnicity, gender, sexuality, or even physical or mental ability, let alone discuss what an accurate representation of any of these selves might look like on the page. And the more you and I think about identity, the more we might discover that cultural appropriation is less a question of "staying in one's lane," as one of your classmates put it, than an evolving conversation we must have around privilege and aesthetic fashion in literary practice.

In a literary world dominated by both writing-workshop culture and social media, many writers hone their aesthetics under the intoxicating influence of ego and shame: how to win your instructor's or classmates' approval, how to avoid vilification on Twitter, how to get a book published before you turn twenty-five. But ego and shame reject nuance in favor of outrage or thinkpieces gone viral on the Internet, which purport to offer guidance but more often than not mine our own latent seams of insecurity, bolstering the suspicion that, no matter what choice we make, what ideas we agree with and what writers we strive to imitate, that choice is always wrong. It's another reason I think our class discussion about cultural appropriation felt so fraught; not only do we each see very smart people around us quick and free to judge, we see them quick to make these judgments public, and to make their object of judgment—ourselves, potentially—the object of derision.

I'm not here to judge. I don't want to revisit the successes or failures of your poem, X, but to examine with you the strategies employed by other writers who've written outside their own identities. I want to do justice to your question, which asks me to consider what literary practices constitute cultural appropriation, and whether such practices are always wrong. I want to think carefully about why some works of literature feel exploitative while others don't. I want to talk about literary prestige and cultural power, and I want to consider how racism and prejudice affect our very idea of the "free" or "human" imagination. Most important, I want to offer you some tools to answer this question for yourself, because the fact is you might reject some or all of my arguments, and I think these disagreements, while uncomfortable, are ultimately good, and will be returned to as you develop as an artist. The ideas that I express here, X, are ideas of a moment; I have not always held these ideas myself, and I may not continue to hold them as the world in which we live revises itself. You, too, will change your mind. Because the questions you and I have around cultural appropriation cannot be asked and answered only once: they must be asked and answered every year, every decade we work as writers. Power isn't static. Race and gender aren't static. Nothing about our identities, our political presence, and social meaning in the world remains stable. So long as we change, the questions we hold around representation change with us, and what we take as fundamental aesthetic precepts now will be unfashionable, even embarrassing, to future generations.

This is something I experienced myself firsthand the other week, during a class on meter I'd been teaching for another seminar. That day I brought into class a poem once popular in the late '90s titled "Effort at Speech," about a mugging its author, William Meredith, either imagined or experienced. The poem is written in sapphics, a hugely difficult meter in English to pull off due to its cascade of interlocking dactyls and trochees, which is why I'd wanted to show it to the students. I hadn't read this poem myself in more than twenty years, so I was a little taken aback when reading it again with fresh eyes. Here is the poem in its entirety:

Climbing the stairway gray with urban midnight,
Cheerful, venial, ruminating pleasure,
Darkness takes me, an arm around my throat and
                    Give me your wallet.

Fearing cowardice more than other terrors,
Angry I wrestle with my unseen partner,
Caught in a ritual not of our making,
                    panting like spaniels.

Bold with adrenaline, mindless, shaking,
God damn it, no! I rasp at him behind me,
Wrenching the leather from his grasp. It
                    breaks like a wishbone,

So that departing (routed by my shouting,
Not by my strength or inadvertent courage)
Half the papers lending me a name are
                    gone with him nameless.

Only now turning, I see a tall boy running,
Fifteen, sixteen, dressed thinly for the weather.
Reaching the streetlight he turns a brown face briefly
                    phrased like a question.

I like a questioner watch him turn the corner
Taking the answer with him, or his half of it.
Loneliness, not a sensible emotion,
                    breathes hard on the stairway.

Walking homeward I fraternize with shadows,
Zigzagging with them where they flee the streetlights,
Asking for trouble, asking for the message
                trouble had sent me.

All fall down has been scribbled on the street in
Garbage and excrement: so much for the vision
Others taunt me with, my untimely humor,
                so much for cheerfulness.

Next time don't wrangle, give the boy the money,
Call across chasms what the world you know is.
Luckless and lied to, how can a child master
                human decorum?

Next time a switchblade, somewhere he is thinking,
I should have killed him and took the lousy wallet.
Reading my cards, he feels a surge of anger
                blind as my shame.

Error from Babel mutters in the places,
Cities apart, where now we word our failures:
Hatred and guilt have left us without language
                who might have held discourse.

Meredith's speaker is presumably White, his teenage assailant Black. I say "presumably" because Meredith himself was White, and because the narrator focuses on his assailant's "brown face," while at the same characterizing his assailant's world through images

of darkness that symbolize menace, social decay, or violence—
something the speaker imagines as essentially in opposition to the
world the speaker knows. The teenager isn't even portrayed as fully
human until late in the poem; instead, he's metonymically represented by darkness itself, which grabs Meredith's speaker around
the throat, the two men now "[c]aught in a ritual not of [their] making." The suggestion is that the mugging both violates and fulfills
the rules of a larger social order, in which Black or brown male teen-
agers target wealthier Whites who've wandered into their territory,
here a description of streets with the words "*All fall down . . .* scribbled with / [g]arbage and excrement."

The mugging also appears to unleash some menace latent in
Meredith's speaker who, missing the papers "lending [him] a name,"
now abandons his formerly "cheerful, venial" attitude that his
middle-class status keeps at bay in favor now of "fratern[izing] with
shadows/ [z]igzagging with them where they flee the streetlights, /
asking for trouble." After the attack, Meredith's speaker fantasizes
that he might run into the boy again, this time giving him his wallet, perhaps as a condescending gesture of sympathy for the boy's
condition, which the speaker imagines as "luckless and lied to," the
teen someone who hasn't "master[ed] / human decorum." The teen's
envisioned response to the after-effects of the attack, however, is to
plot further violence. "Next time a switchblade," the speaker imagines the teen muttering, wishing he'd killed his victim.

You can see that the poem is filled with sentimental racism; the
speaker's wistful hope that, if only they might speak, he and the
teenager could see each other's humanity is everywhere undercut
by the poem's imagery. Though Meredith makes a metaphor of the
wallet torn in half by the two men—victim and assailant here share

a single identity—that metaphor is weakened by the fact that the social meaning of darkness and whiteness are in opposition to each other. If the teenager's world is one of darkness, garbage, decay, and incoherence, the White speaker's world is one of fragile pleasure and decorous, expertly polished language. Black violence threatens to disrupt these pleasures, even to erase the speaker's own identity, so that the White man takes on the assumed characteristics of his assailant. Whiteness and Blackness are not part of the same human identity; instead, they represent different ideas of humanness itself: one marked by arbitrary violence and speechlessness, one defined by empathy, art, and civility.

My students, unsurprisingly, were nonplussed. "This is *racist*," one declared, a charge I agreed with, chagrinned, remembering only how I'd once admired Meredith's dexterous rhythms, the deft ways in which form and content—the breathless mugging, the poem's clipped, dactylic rhythms—snapped together. How had I, a college junior, missed the poem's undercurrents? As a mixed-race person, shouldn't the poem's racism always have been obvious to me? I scanned my students' tense faces. I could see them wondering whether I had brought this poem to them because I'd missed its ugliness; worse, whether I liked it. Did I like it? Had I seen Meredith's racism when I first read it, and not only absorbed his poem's condescension but approved of it? I was twenty-one the year I first read it, the same year the Rodney King riots engulfed L.A., and though I, like many, believed the cops who beat King should have been imprisoned, I remember also watching the video footage on TV of buildings and cars burning with fascinated horror. I remember interviews with Korean American shopkeepers, many who looked like my Chinese family members, sympathetic to the shock and fear they expressed over losing their stores. My own racial background and safety among the police helped me to see one story behind the news, but not all of them. For me, the riots seemed out of proportion to the crime, because I had no awareness of the long and brutal history of extrajudicial violence against African Americans by police, violence that had only amplified during the early 1980s. I had no sense this event wasn't a spontaneous act of greed or grievance but the result of profound injustice reinforced over generations of violence against Black people, and I had no appreciation for the ways my voyeurism had been primed by television shows that depicted Black men as criminals. To me, reading "Effort at Speech" at age twenty-one, Meredith's attitude toward his assailant hadn't seemed racist, but generous.

Of course, I am now twenty-eight years older than when I first read that poem. My understanding of the Rodney King riots is different from my reaction to them as a college student, just as my understanding of poetry and race, and of what constitutes generosity in a work of art has deepened and altered. When I show you "Effort at Speech" now, I suspect you see in its paternalistic failures what I have learned to see in it. Like many of my students, I suspect you've taken courses that delve into race and gender theory. You've watched the national news, and you've seen the deadly effects of the language we still use to depict people of color in our culture. You've been taught by teachers like me, who changed your curriculum so that more writers and identities are represented in the ever-expanding, ever-debated list that comprises what we call a literary canon. The result is that we both now recognize Meredith's stereotypes for what they are; the world in which this poem and its sentiments could be lauded has changed.

Fair enough. But what, then, do I as a teacher and you as a reader do with Meredith's poem? By my ceasing to teach it and you refusing to read it, do we together consign Meredith to obscurity? Or do we attempt to rescue his poem through formal analysis, abandoning its values in favor of studying Meredith's complex rhythms? And how could we possibly separate form from content without also implicitly reinforcing Meredith's sentimental racism? Because to isolate poetic technique in this manner would naïvely privilege artistry, and here explicitly White artistry, over real problems of racial representation.

Or is there another option? Do I, as a teacher, let Meredith's poem become something both more difficult and more instructive to us both, by using "Effort at Speech" as a vehicle for a conversation we might have around the co-construction of Whiteness and Blackness in literature? Might the sapphic form become a way to discuss not just Meredith's form, but how Whiteness historically has required ideas of "the Other" for its own systematic development?

As a teacher and a writer, I know what my answer to these questions would be. But I don't know what your answers are, X, even as I imagine that whatever answer you give now will, like my reactions to "Effort at Speech," evolve over time. When it comes to race and representation, you and I are trying to make amends for the sins of our shared past while also working with still-incomplete knowledge, both about ourselves and about how we understand who, or what, constitutes "the Other." There is always some key just beyond our training and comprehension, which is not to say that you and I don't see the effects of racial, ethnic, gender, and physical difference in the world. We see and experience the practical effects of our identities all the time, but we don't completely understand how to situate them in language. When I look to the past for models, I can see that

Shakespeare wrote as a Moor, as a Jewish merchant, as women, as a disabled king. I can see that Twain wrote about a runaway slave and that Faulkner wrote from the perspective of a Black female servant, a mentally disabled man, and an aging woman. I can study these works, I can admire them, and I can also see how these works might fail in some critical way in representing these identities as you and I might understand them now. The past offers us examples, but it doesn't offer many perfect ones, and it never presents us the automatic right to continue in a particular aesthetic vein.

So when you ask me for an essay about cultural appropriation, I understand you are asking for something other than a glib answer as to whether you can or can't write from the perspective of someone unlike yourself. You don't really want an authority to consign works of literature into simple but often dishonest categories of "right" or "wrong." I think you're asking a more complicated set of questions around how we socially understand and also creatively represent the complexities inherent to our identities, and how much compassion, curiosity, and empathy might factor into crafting literary characters. You recognize that literature, at heart, is alchemical, even transgressive, and that as readers we are porous to its effects; we can be profoundly changed or moved by human creativity. We can also be wounded by it. Thus you are not just asking for an essay to provide you with models to study or avoid, but to show you how you and I might imagine our relationship to the past, while using that relationship to forge progressive change in the future.

With these questions in mind, I'm going to write the essay I haven't found, by thinking through my answers with you in a series of letters, first by examining what constitutes appropriation, as well as racial and cultural identity, and then by looking at how writers have chosen to represent these identities on the page. If a poem I read in the 1990s now seems antiquated with regards to its racial politics, it will be too easy for you to discern the flaws in even older works, so for this reason I'm going to spend more time thinking about literature and some works of popular art from the twentieth and twenty-first centuries than further in the past, because their ideas about race and appropriation are closer to ours, more powerfully expressed in our current aesthetic DNA. And of course, the works I select here won't be the only ones in this period that have employed appropriation. I look at these works because in them I find some useful lesson that *I* have learned as a reader and writer, and because my examination might serve as a critical rubric for you to apply to other texts, including your own.

I am also writing to invite you to articulate your own ethics around appropriation as you read these letters; I ask you to consider for yourself the usefulness or vacuity of the term "cultural appropriation." I've often wondered whether writers and readers react, instinctively, so angrily to the thought of appropriation because the word itself denotes only the act of taking. What if we were to complicate the kinds and types of appropriation that artists engage in by specifically delineating them or, better yet, separating out examples of harmful or racist appropriation from those of compassionate or intellectually engaged cultural *approximation*? What, too, if we were to examine the ways that all of us are implicated in acts of appropriation, both as agents but also as subjects? By teasing out the differences between types of artistic appropriation, you and I can have a clearer understanding of what's at stake when someone accuses a work of being culturally appropriative. Not all works that engage in appropriation are automatically racist, and not all works of appropriation present us with the same ethical problems.

Finally, I'm asking you to recognize that, regardless of how you and I come to define the practice of appropriation, there will be readers who eschew it for historical reasons around how people of color have been represented in Western culture. The fact is, X, people's actual bodies, identities, and artifacts have been commodified by powerful groups and institutions. For these readers, the question of creativity will always take second place to the enduring history of colonialism, which means that for them appropriation is an inherently political, not only literary, practice.

These readers' disagreements do not mean that they are against free speech, but that they are interested in larger questions around freedom, which is the right of particular communities to control their stories and to demand that the majority no longer has automatic access to any subject matter it likes. This freedom may at times feel to you like censorship. But censorship occurs when someone, usually a government, agent of the state, or a powerful institution, actively suppresses information or media. Censorship is a programmatic response to speech that offends, that is perceived as volatile, false, or harmful to a community's security. In this nation with its liberal publishing laws and its constitutionally protected freedom of speech, with its myriad self-publishing houses and blogs and websites, only you have the power to censor yourself. My criticism, your classmates' disdain, the agent's reluctance to represent you, your editor's ambivalence—all these things can be navigated if you so desire. As you've seen yourself in class when someone questions the nature of your work, that's not censorship but criticism.

Likewise, another reader's sensitivity to appropriation is not an automatic mark of her brainwashing, a sign that she would perhaps flag for binning such works as *To Kill a Mockingbird* or *The Adven-*

tures of Huckleberry Finn, as if these texts were perfect and inalterable. Writers know all texts are alterable. There is no perfect book: a work can be innovative and culturally appropriative at once, historically important and also racist, beautifully composed and morally repellant. That, to me, is the complexity that accompanies and defines human works of art.

The reality is that there is no one set of questions about appropriation that, if answered clearly and correctly, will grant you universal permission, just as there are no political sentiments or empathetic desires you harbor that will produce unassailable results.

I was reminded of this a few days ago, listening to a fellow poet's anecdote about an incident he recently experienced in a buffet line. A number of strangers had gathered around this poet to talk about food. The strangers were White, many from the same family, and they were all talking about what they wanted to eat. When they got to the watermelon plate, the older White woman next to the poet, Jericho, who's African American, admitted to her daughter that she'd never liked watermelon. Then, to be friendly, she turned to Jericho and began to ask if he liked watermelon, at which point the daughter burst out, "Oh my God, Mommy, *don't*." The mother, realizing at that exact moment how her question might be taken, blushed and fell silent.

All this Jericho watched, while also pretending not to see or hear any of it. He had, he told me, already decided that once these strangers reached the watermelon plate, the conversation would likely come to such a head, and that—for these strangers' sakes, if not for his own—it would be better for him to pretend he couldn't hear them speaking at all.

Now Jericho understands that the White woman didn't ask

the question to be racist, but as a Black man he would still prefer not to have his initial conversation with a White stranger begin with a question about whether he likes watermelon. It didn't matter whether the woman "meant anything" by her question, but her daughter's interruption was a reminder that watermelon has a symbolic history behind it, a history of which the mother should have been more alert in the context of her wanting to engage Jericho in conversation. The mother's friendly curiosity was not an excuse to say anything she wanted to Jericho. Instead, perhaps, her desire to speak with Jericho should have been based first not on her interest about him, but on her concern for protecting his dignity.

When it comes to writing about or through the lives of others, we have to begin with the desire to respect each other's dignity and difference from ourselves, and this requires an understanding of the history of the individuals we wish to represent. And we also have to begin with the understanding of empathy's limits: we are not all of us the same, though we share profound similarities, and certainly feel the same emotions.

Parsing this fine line between difference and similarity, self and other, metaphor and stereotype is not only the activity that constitutes appropriation but literature itself. So perhaps the final request you're making of me, X, is to examine with you the competing, and sometimes conflicting values we hold about imaginative writing. What relationship do you enter into with a text when you read? How much do you shape, and how much are you shaped by, the interpretation of the poems and stories you consume? If, like writing, reading is an active skill, one that demands perceptiveness, practice, and, yes, a desire to protect the essential dignity of people who are figured in language, what are the ethical risks *and* rewards to reading works that are appropriative? In other words, X, what do you desire when you come to a work of literature?

All these questions lie inside your one request to "get it right." And with these questions in mind, let's begin.

LETTER TWO

Setting the Terms

D<small>ear</small> X:

The first thing to understand is that the term "appropriation" simply means the use of a preexisting object or image that you've repurposed without fundamentally changing it. Appropriation is an accepted, widespread practice in both music and art, and it's also commonly used in literature. Before I talk about specific works of literature, however, I want to talk about instances of appropriation you might have experienced in popular culture at large, so that I can show you some of the complexities hidden within the general concept of cultural appropriation.

In music, appropriation forms the aesthetic basis of hip-hop, which samples from other artists and street sounds as references that provide the listener musical texture and ambience, which you can see in tracks by artists like Nas, Dopp Gang, Kanye West, or

De La Soul. In art, you see appropriation in works by Pablo Picasso, Andy Warhol, Marcel Duchamp, Joseph Cornell, Jeff Koons, and Robert Rauschenberg. Appropriation in art changes the object's meaning by changing the context through which the viewer sees, hears, or reads the object itself. The urinal in the bathroom stall, for example, is a toilet; on the wall of an art museum, it's conceptual art. In literature, those contextual changes are sometimes harder to accept, because as readers we've been conditioned to value stories that are fundamentally tied to authorship, thus to specific identities. No one, however, is the author of a urinal or a soup can; these are mass-produced objects meant to be used by everyone.

Perhaps, reading these letters, you suspect you've already come across an example of appropriation. Perhaps you heard other students from my seminar arguing about Meredith's poem, so you know that I've transformed part of that classroom event into a literary analogy to suit my discussion with you. That's part of the power I possess as a writer: I take things presented to me in one context, whether literary, personal, or historical, and rewrite or reimagine them for my own ends. I doubt you saw my use of that classroom event as any kind of cultural theft, understanding it to be something more akin to anecdote or embellishment. As the scholar Pascal Nicklas notes in his book *Adaptation and Cultural Appropriation*, "appropriate" carries within it the Latin word "*proprius*," which means "something that is characteristic, that is part of oneself." In the case of my class seminar, I've demonstrated that one of its essential characteristics is its public nature; in that, I might use and alter its facts to suit a larger narrative purpose.

Literary theorists call this kind of appropriation "adaptation," and you see this in literature all the time.

When adaptation occurs in literature, it's usually when a writer refashions for her own original work particular artistic elements of another work, such as plot, theme, literary or technical devices, subject matters, or symbolic motifs. Shakespeare, in his play *Titus Andronicus*, appropriates Ovid's own retelling of the ancient Greek myth of Philomela. Margaret Atwood appropriates the plot and subject matter of Shakespeare's play *The Tempest* in her novel *Hag Seed*, just as she appropriates the motifs of Grimm's fairy tales in her collection of short stories, *The Robber Bride*. Derek Walcott appropriates *The Odyssey* for his own epic poem, *Omeros*, just as Pat Barker appropriates the story of Briseis from *The Iliad* for her novel *The Silence of the Girls*. Conceptual poets like Kenneth Goldsmith and Craig Dworkin copy news articles and weather and traffic reports word for word as a way of frustrating the limits we have conventionally set between "creative" and "uncreative" writing. Postmodern writers like David Shields (or T. S. Eliot) might appropriate the language of a variety of texts by collaging them into a new but unified literary work, as Shields does in his manifesto *Reality Hunger*, and Eliot does in "The Waste Land." George R. R. Martin appropriates the events of historical accounts of the Hundred Years' War in his series *Game of Thrones*. And every year, dozens of novels and films appropriate *Pride and Prejudice* in an attempt to re-create, and reimagine, the world of Jane Austen.

All of these works are examples of literary adaptation. The critic Julie Sanders, in her book *Adaptation and Appropriation*, calls adaptation and appropriation "side by side" practices, with adaptation defined as work that's "closer in degree" to the original text or source than one that's merely appropriative. According to Sanders, an adapted work gestures to a relationship with a specific source text that allows readers to identify what she calls "movements of prox-imation or cross-generic interpretation." Appropriation, however, requires comprehensive rethinking of the original work's expression and meaning. It is, as she says, "a more decisive journey away from the informing source into a wholly new cultural product and domain." Basically, adapted works derive their pleasure from the fact that we recognize the original source. Appropriative works don't require that we recognize these sources at all. Appropriation may be part of adaptation, but while they are similar, the two are different from each other based upon the degree of difference from their original source.

Adaptation, in this sense, shades uncomfortably into plagia-rism, and here you should look to the American University School of Communication's Center for Social Media "Code of Best Practices in Fair Use for Poetry" to clarify questions you might have about the transformational purpose of appropriated material. Simply put, is your work using the original source for a different purpose than the original, or does it repeat the work word for word or structure for structure, to re-create "the same intent and value as the original"? Appropriative and adapted works, even as they mine another source for inspiration, work toward the goal of producing their own origi-nal meanings and products. They also make a nod—whether explic-itly, through clear attribution; or implicitly, through recognizable symbols, titles, and phrases—to their original sources.

There are readers who might disdain adaptations as much as appropriations, and likely for some of the same reasons, which is the privilege writers place on originality and also the connection they make between authorship and intellectual property. For writers, a published creative work is property that can be owned, sold, and purchased, and it possesses material as well as cultural value.

But what about artistic elements that we see as tied to specific cultures but aren't practically able to be sold or purchased, like songs or religious myths? If certain stories or aesthetic elements are associated with a culture, or if a culture argues that it collectively created these aesthetic elements or stories, does it follow that the culture then legally owns these elements? Sadly, copyright law focuses on specific or concrete artistic works and the execution of an idea. Cultural control of stories and literary motifs is an issue of ethical, not legal ownership. Stories belong to cultures based on recitation, practice, shared knowledge, and memory. A writer may want to keep her stories within the boundaries of her own community, but she can't practically—or easily—enforce this desire in the courts. But even if there is no legal claim a culture might make against an author, that doesn't mean it doesn't have an ethical claim. Ethical artists avoid appropriation not out of fear of being sued but out of fear of harming others through insensitive depictions.

In general, an appropriative artistic act can include taking a material object from one context and using it in another, or performing certain songs and stories originally authored by another artist, or using artistic elements from another artwork in your own art. These, however, are not the kind of appropriative practices I suspect you're asking about. You aren't worried about artistic influence or postmodern collage or adaptation so much as about what constitutes cultural appropriation.

As many of your classmates noted in workshop, cultural appropriation occurs when an artist, or collector, appropriates objects or aesthetic practices from a culture or community different from her own for her own use. This may include being inspired by stylistic elements or stories from another culture's artworks, but it also includes collecting and exhibiting ritual objects from other cultures, such as a natural history museum's display of indigenous people's skeletons. It also includes the taking of another culture's artworks wholesale as one's own, which is what the British Museum did with the Elgin marbles or the Musée du Quai Branly did with African objects taken from France's former African colonies.

The philosopher James O. Young, in his book *Cultural Appropriation and the Arts*, breaks down cultural appropriation into two general categories: subject appropriation and content appropriation. Content appropriation may also be called motif appropriation, and it occurs when artists from one culture are influenced by artists from another but without creating works in the original artists' exact style. You can see this with Paul Simon, who uses musical elements gleaned from South African townships on his album *Graceland*, or in Picasso's *Les Demoiselles d'Avignon*, which is influenced by African carved masks. In literature, you see this in Marlon James's *Black Leopard, Red Wolf*, which takes on the Akan people's Anansi myths.

Subject appropriation, however, occurs when a writer depicts a real culture or community other than her own, whether by focusing her work on particular events, people, or practices that exist within that culture or community, or by writing in the voice of a specific member of that community. We see this in Gauguin's Tahiti paintings, for example; or in *Kim*, when Rudyard Kipling writes from the perspective of a young Indian boy.

Subject appropriation is what the writer Lionel Shriver defended in her impassioned and angrily received keynote address at the 2016 Brisbane Writers Festival. In it, Shriver declared that she was "hopeful the concept of 'cultural appropriation' is a passing fad," insisting that all fiction was at heart inauthentic, and that it was both the writer's right and duty to imagine the lives of those different from themselves: what we call "appropriation," then, wasn't theft but the essence of fiction itself. Shriver's argument duplicates (or perhaps appropriates) Margaret Drabble's 2004 argument that "appropriation is what novelists do. Whatever we write is, knowingly or unknowingly, a borrowing. Nothing comes from nowhere."

Drabble, who created Guyanese and Jewish characters for her novel *The Witch of Exmore* and an eighteenth-century Korean royal protagonist for *The Red Queen*, later walked these comments back in a 2017 *Publishers Weekly* article, saying, "You can't just barge in there and assume you have got the right to tell other people's stories. You have to react sensitively to other people." Drabble's hesitation does not seem to be shared by Shriver, however; two years after her talk in Brisbane, in the March issue of *Prospect*, Shriver amplified her argument, insisting that our "call out" culture was slowly creating a literature that would ultimately be "timid, homogenous, and dreary."

"The whole apparatus of delivering literature to its audience [now]," Shriver wrote, "is signaling an intention to subject fiction to rigid ideological purity tests, unrelated to artistry, excellence and even entertainment, that miss the point of what our books are for." For Shriver, to concern ourselves with "political correctness" doesn't just produce art that bores, it narrows the writer's artistic vision, shrinking the reader's own capacity for imaginative empathy as a result.

As you might imagine, Shriver's comments outraged a lot of people, and it didn't help that she delivered her remarks wearing a Mexican sombrero. But while the public backlash to Shriver's speech is understandable, it's something that, for the moment, I want to set aside. You may take issue with Shriver's claims, but it is a fact that appropriation *is* deeply tied to artistic practice, whether through the adaptation and appropriation of another artist's content or through the appropriation of cultural subjects themselves. One of the reasons that Shriver's claims sounded so outrageous was that she herself bundled together a variety of appropriative practices into the same category of "cultural appropriation," thus to defend rewriting *King Lear* was potentially also to defend the writing of *Uncle Remus*. But there's a difference between adapting a widely shared story and the burlesquing of a particular artifact we consider unique to a specific culture, and that difference might best be articulated by the legal scholar Susan Scafidi in her book *Who Owns Culture? Appropriation and Authenticity in American Law*, who argues that cultural appropriation is the taking of someone else's "intellectual property, traditional knowledge, cultural expressions, or artifacts" in order to *"suit [our] own tastes, express [our] own individuality, or simply make a profit"* (italics mine).

It's this combined problem of cultural privilege, profit, and self-aggrandizement that must be considered when we appropriate items from other cultures. It's one thing to buy and display a Berber basket purchased during your trip to Morocco. That's a form of cultural appreciation for an object the Berbers gave explicit permission to sell. It's another thing entirely to secretly photograph a sacred Hopi ritual and publish it in a book of photos under your own name. This is no longer cultural influence or admiration, but theft. And this theft also returns us to the problem of how certain artists and institutions have materially profited from the cultural products of other communities. When Shriver argues that appropriation is what writers do, she conveniently forgets that certain writers have made money off the cultural narratives and artifacts of communities of color, as the White mystery writer Tony Hillerman did when writing about the Navajo Tribal Police. When using African artifacts as inspiration for his work, Picasso was the one who became rich and famous, not the original African artists.

Perhaps, X, you might point out that this is a problem of luck more than it is an ethical issue inherent to cultural appropriation. There is no automatic guarantee, for instance, that an artist who appropriates the motifs and subjects of another culture will become as commercially lauded as a Hillerman or Picasso. If a writer rewrites the stories of another culture and makes no money from it, shouldn't that be taken into account? But while a small-press poet may not individually have as much cultural power as a Picasso, she is also part of a larger, and longer, narrative of how Western cultures have represented non-White communities. In that, her appropriation becomes a problem of history more than a simple problem of respective earnings. You and I are individuals, but we also come from and represent powerful nations that have materially profited from and profoundly harmed the cultures we are now influenced by.

Likewise, Shriver forgets that not all appropriations receive an equal amount of cultural attention. When a White writer takes on the stories of a non-Western culture or a community of color and her work is lauded while the writer of color's narrative gets critically ignored, it is the White writer's depiction of that community that then risks becoming the authenticating narrative for the reading public. Thus how we judge appropriative works cannot solely be determined by economics or by the legal and creative freedom we have to be influenced by cultures other than our own; otherwise, we ignore how the most enduring harm done to communities of color might not be the loss of money by particular individuals but the dissemination of painful stereotypes about their members.

If we can't keep motifs and stories within our own cultures either legally or practically, then the practice of appropriation becomes an individual choice with larger, historical implications. I'll speak about this at greater length in the next letter, but for now a better question to ask yourself than whether or not content appropriation is racist is to ask in what ways a particular artist's appropriation has been benefitted by racist policies and beliefs, and in what ways it speaks back to them. Oftentimes, you'll find that an appropriative work does both at once. Paul Simon's 1986 album *Graceland*, for example, is the result of his close work with South African musicians who created the riffs and rhythms he later curated into songs. Simon's work with these artists violated the international boycott established by the UN Anti-Apartheid Committee, unsettling some in the group Artists United Against Apartheid, who thought Simon had put the ambitions of a few artists above the protest itself. *Graceland* helped these artists, well known in their home country, establish a broader, international fame as well as a platform that increased anti-apartheid sentiment. It also gave Simon the lion's share of the attention and profits.

All of these problems, X, swirl inside our feelings about cultural appropriation. In its social connotation, you and I understand that cultural appropriation means someone with more cultural capital and power has taken the objects, artifacts, and stories of someone with less cultural capital and power without permission and for her own benefit. According to the legal definition, anyone can commit an act of cultural appropriation; a Japanese singer riffing on "Yankee Doodle Dandy," for example, is committing an act of cultural appropriation. Today, however, you and I generally mean that someone White and from the West has taken an object or narrative from someone non-White, and possibly not from the West. In that, the term "cultural appropriation" carries with it the distinct whiff of colonialism.

UNDERSTANDING THE IMPACT OF COLONIALISM

Based on my definition of content and subject appropriation and adaptation, you may wonder whether all texts are equally available for our creative use. The answer to that relies upon a more nuanced understanding of how the history of colonialism has influenced the reception of texts in our reading canon. This came up in a discussion I had with my father when I told him I was writing you these letters about cultural appropriation. My father reacted in much the same way that Lionel Shriver might, by launching into a list of classic works that have appropriated characters and stories from cultures not their own. He even brought up *The Iliad*, arguing that if we have no problem with authors appropriating Greek culture, why should we be upset about a White man rewriting, say, the sixteenth-century Chinese classic *Journey to the West*?

First, we have to remember that *The Iliad* was likely multiply authored: "Homer" is a series of poets who have, over time, created one of the first hybrid, polyvocal texts in existence. Second, *The Iliad* has been translated and reimagined and performed so many different times and ways, and in so many different contexts, it has become a cultural palimpsest, not a reflection of any one particular culture. Its repeated exposure and rewriting means that its ownership has gradually been removed from a particular culture, even as my father or I may trot it out as a symbol of that culture.

In other words, many of the ways in which we've translated, read, and taught *The Iliad* are based on our changing historical formula-

tions of "Ancient Greece" and "The West," thus the value of its cultural products themselves is always in flux. In that, the text is not
owned by or even only reflective of one particular city-state at one
particular moment in time: we are always inventing and rewriting
The Iliad each time we translate it. *The Iliad*, in that sense, has been
jettisoned from its original time and place; it is now a text *whose use is
to be appropriated*. It is the same with Ovid's *Metamorphoses*, which
became the basis of thousands of different rewritings, from Chaucer
to Shakespeare to Keats to Ted Hughes. Ovid's *Metamorphoses* is a
"Roman" text in much the same way that Shakespeare's *King Lear* is
an "English" text: it has its origins in a culture and place and region,
but it no longer belongs only to that culture, place, or region. These
stories have become part of global culture at large; you and I are taught
to assign them the value of being "archetypal" or "universal," which
means, at some level, we have de-authored and de-cultured them.

You might argue that "de-authoring" and "de-culturing" are
forms of privilege that befall primarily White or Western male
authors. Part of the reason for this is because what we claim as universal is mistakenly categorized as "raceless," which codes as White.
As an unmarked category, Whiteness resides at the center of our literary canon and so it is unsurprising when, with White-as-raceless
set as our default reading mode, how and what we teach often inad-
vertently replicates classical hierarchies. When I tell you that all
texts and cultures can be appropriated, I overlook the ways in which
certain texts have entered and formed our conventional ideas of the
literary canon, and which texts have been left out. When my father
says, for example, that Shakespeare took Italian stories as his own,
this does not culturally disenfranchise the Italians, who have profoundly shaped our ideas of the European West, and who have a

wide and varied literature of their own. But so do the Chinese, and if a White American man from, say, Oklahoma wants to rewrite *The Journey to the West*, what's wrong with that?

Nothing, except for the fact that in Europe and America, we've filtered a lot of our images of the East through the lens of what the scholar Edward Said called Orientalism, which is, as he said, "a way of coming to terms with [the Middle East and Asia] based on the Orient's special place in European Western experience." The Middle East and Asia, both sites of some of western Europe's earliest colonies, became emblematic of western Europe's most enduring image of "the Other": primitive, violent, irrational, radical, sexually suspect, autocratic, and duplicitous.

Orientalism affected not only our political and even geographical representation of East Asian, South Asian, and also Middle Eastern cultures, but also our cultural and artistic representations of "The Orient," which means that even though the Japanese, Chinese, Koreans, Vietnamese, and Indians all have rich, distinct, and varied literatures, our Western imagination of the East remains limited by the lens of Orientalism that exists to support our own cultural dominance. The theory of Orientalism provides a good model for how we have responded to and absorbed literature from other cultures around the world, including African nations, as our lens has been distorted by how we've historically justified slavery. Thus you can appropriate a French text and not have it touch the same nerves as appropriating a West African one, since at certain points in history, our nations have literally bought and sold West Africans.

But I argue that this process of de-authoring and de-culturing, even if it does not happen automatically for all authors and texts, *is possible* for all authors and texts. Time allows for it; globalization and cosmopolitan reading practices practically ensure it. The fact that *Journey to the West* has not been popularly appropriated in America (other than Maxine Hong Kingston's *Tripmaster Monkey*) might say more about American education and reading habits than about the exclusive cultural ownership of *Journey to the West*. In Asia and Southeast Asia, *Journey to the West* has already been turned into Japanese anime, Australian TV shows, South Korean movies, Taiwanese plays, and Singaporean musicals. My father is right: *Journey to the West* can be and has been appropriated, at least across Asia, where it has achieved the same cultural status there as a Homeric epic or Shakespearean drama here. Our reluctance to appropriate it in the United States primarily reflects our Eurocentric view of what constitutes an iconic text. But if Kurosawa can appropriate *Macbeth* for his epic *Ran*, there is no reason why American writers, of all identities, cannot also adapt the plot and themes of *Journey to the West*. What that adaptation would require, however, is a sensitive understanding of how the West's imagination has been shaped by its colonial thinking of the East. This is something I believe we can achieve because I'm a teacher, and if I didn't believe that education changed people, then I'm clearly in the wrong business. But American appropriations of *Journey to the West* are coming and, I would argue, it will be an important sign about the changes in our imaginative relationship with Asia when they do.

APPROPRIATION AS HARM: REFINING THE TERMS

Based on what I've written so far, you might see that appropriation in literature is neither an unusual practice nor one that's always and inherently wrong. But I also noted that appropriation can cause harm, whether through cultural theft that leads to material loss, or through the proliferation of damaging stereotypes. This is why I believe we might, in classroom discussions, reconsider and refine our terms once more. You and I might be able to differentiate more usefully between appropriative works that harm another culture and appropriative works that simply write outside the boundaries of the writer's own identity if we did not, like Shriver, lump together all appropriative practices into the same category. I myself use the term "cultural appropriation" specifically to suggest a work that's bound up in the production and dissemination of negative, if also unconscious, stereotypes of another group or culture, and the specific terms "subject" and "content appropriation" for works that are attentively influenced by other cultures, or include nuanced non-White or non-Western characters. But what if, for works that appropriate respectfully, we came up with an entirely new terminology, perhaps something like "transcultural dialogue," "cultural homage," or even "cultural approximation"?

The question is, what constitutes respectful and harmful forms of appropriation?

A few months ago on Twitter, where human kindness goes to die, a story circulated about a Utah teen who went to her prom dressed in a cheongsam. The response online in America was generally one of outrage: the teen was White, suburban, and middle class, and she had no ties to or apparent knowledge of China. The Americans' outrage, interestingly, was not shared online by many Chinese readers, who also took to Twitter saying they found it adorable that a young American woman would find something from their culture beautiful enough to wear to her own prom, and if culture was so particular and distinct, was it wrong for Chinese men to arrive at work wearing Western-style suits or Chinese women to get married in white dresses?

Before reading the story, I was generally on the side of the Chinese. After seeing the photographs, I was on the side of the Americans.

The first photos showed a young woman dressed in a red, gold, and black cheongsam cycling through the usual, parentally commanded poses with her friends, each girl smiling, her date's arm slung around her waist. The last photo, however, showed the girl and her friends all in a half-crouch, their arms spread wide and palms pressed together in that demure prayer-greeting gesture you might find in some dyspeptic high school production of *The King and I*.

With that photo, and that gesture, the girl revealed that, to her, the dress was in fact not just a dress, it was an artifact that came attached to a particular culture, one she found as appealing as the dress, but one she had also gotten wrong. If she'd worn the dress as simply another dress, it would have been an example of respectful appropriation. But the girl changed what was a cultural artifact into an Orientalist fantasy, and by doing this turned the dress into an example of cultural appropriation.

If only she'd just stood and smiled. She would have revealed the cheongsam to be what it has, over time, become: a material object that suggests a specific culture, but is no longer the requirement of that culture, itself influenced by cosmopolitan dressing habits and cultural exchange, to possess or wear.

Of course, by this same logic, X, you might think that Pharrell Williams wearing a warrior bonnet for the cover of *Elle UK* would also be acceptable. It's a piece of clothing he dons, and he attempts no particularly "Indian" behaviors for the camera while wearing it. And yet the warrior bonnet is harder to make into a simple material artifact that can be shared across cultures and time because it has, far more so than the cheongsam, which can be worn by every Chinese and Chinese-descended person through the diaspora, a very particular relationship to culture and history. Williams, in defending the photo, argued that he is himself part American Indian. But not every American Indian wears a war bonnet. Not every American Indian *male* wears a war bonnet, either, because it's something that has to be earned, and because the ones who have earned that privilege don't wear it in daily life. The war bonnet is attached to the history of the Plains Indians, many of whom have been in violent conflict with both the U.S. government and one another at different points in time, thus a war bonnet carries very specific tribal, historical, and familial meanings that cannot be cross-culturally absorbed as easily as we can absorb the meanings behind the cheongsam, which is already so transnationally and transculturally shared.

You and I might get upset by Williams wearing a war bonnet for a fashion shoot not because American Indians are less or more empowered than Chinese in our cultural representations, but because the meanings and memory attached to that particular item are more immediately distinct. In other words, X, what people are fighting over aren't the products of culture so much as the historical memories that get attached to them. Music and food and hairstyles, literary forms, and most articles of clothing are and will always be appropriated, repurposed, shared, bought and sold, assimilated and transformed. It may be infuriating to me, it may cause the faceless horde to roil on social media, but it's inevitable. What's not inevitable, however, is playing dress-up with a material object that represents a people who also experienced genocide.

And that's why literary appropriation is trickier for us to deal with than the question of appropriating material products, because literature traffics in memory and history: the two things that most powerfully comprise and contextualize cultural identity. It's also why even the most empathetic writing of race, writing that investigates and sometimes reinvents historical memory, gets particularly tangled even as it attempts to treat the raced identity with respect, because these are the private and culturally defining stories that shape communities. To write into these spaces is to tread on someone else's intimate territory. It is far more invasive than wearing a sari when you aren't South Asian or trying to become a rap singer when you're White and middle class. You and I may partly define ourselves by what we can buy and perform, but ultimately we understand that we can lose these items—that we are, in fact, constantly in the process of losing them, while also purchasing other people's items and suturing them to our own identities—and still feel like ourselves.

I will fight to the death, however, if someone wants to take away my communal memory.

"THE OTHER" AS METAPHOR FOR THE WHITE IMAGINATION

I was thinking about the problems of memory recently while reading about the art world's reactions to Dana Schutz's painting for the 2017 Whitney Biennial, *Open Casket*, which depicts the murdered body of Emmett Till, a Black teenager who, in 1955, had been lynched by Whites who accused him of flirting with a White woman. Till's mother famously requested the open casket so that her son's mutilated face could be seen, and it was, by tens of thousands of people, some of whom also photographed Till and published the images in newspapers. Mamie Till Bradley, Emmett Till's mother, made a conscious decision to make her son's brutal death a public demonstration against the White violence that killed him, and against the White justice system that would neither legally protect her son from such false and racially motivated charges but would later acquit his White killers.

Schutz's decision to paint Till while lying in his casket was considered by many art critics and painters as an act of cultural appropriation. Schutz is White and has no obvious communal or historic claims to paint Till's image, even though some might persuasively argue that Schutz, as a White woman, will always be implicated in America's systemic racism. Schutz's decision to paint Till, who in death became one of the most galvanizing figures of the civil rights movement, may be considered by some as an act of personal reckoning with the violence that undergirds White identity and history, an attempt to meditate upon White America's racism. In that broad sense, Schutz—and any other White American—has some profound cultural relationship to Till's history.

Critics argued that Till's image was not Schutz's to take. But critics of Schutz's painting, by focusing on the issue of cultural ownership, downplay the point of keeping Till's casket open. The power and meaning behind Bradley's decision to display her mutilated son was based on the fact that White Americans at the time had not seen nor looked closely at Black suffering. To close Till's casket would have mimicked the larger cultural closure that White America daily enacted on Black pain. It would have shunted Till to the margins of the nation's consciousness, rendering him further invisible to the justice system and the media. Bradley's decision to keep the casket open was timely, it was contextually grounded, and it took full control of the voyeurism she encouraged, a voyeurism that could only be sanctified and empowered by the fact that it was so specific in its context of witnessing that even the wide reproduction of Till's image in photographs later could not make Till the object of grue-some speculation but a symbol of our national shame.

Whether or not Schutz had any cultural claim to Till's image is, to my mind, beside the point, since her painting disregards the visual message that Bradley understood she'd made. Once Till had been seen in the ways his mother needed him to be seen, to depict his body again and in a different medium would neuter the political focus of our gaze. In Schutz's painting, I no longer see the forces that murdered Till. I see a reproduction of an image I have already seen, thus my attention must be drawn to the gestural qualities that now compose Till. I see Till as saint and wound; I see the blurred smear that constitutes his face, his starched white shirt; the yellow, halo-like circle of silk around his head. My gaze turns to the person who constructed Till and turned him into a metaphor. I do not even see Till himself, who has, under the painter's hand, become an object and a symbol, not a reckoning.

Some might say that Black pain and Black historical subjects should only be owned by Black artists, but I myself am skeptical of both the practical and the ethical implications of that. I think White people have played the central role in the cause and consequences of Black pain, and so a very broad audience shares in the history of Black suffering, even if it does not share or experience that pain at all equally. The greater crime, to me, in painting Emmett Till's body is that it fur-ther dehumanizes Till. In Schutz's painting, he is either a saintly relic or a slab of meat or, weirdly, both; in that, *Open Casket* accidentally mimics the dehumanizing rhetoric used to describe Black bodies.

Schutz's problematic painting recalls for me a poem by the conceptual poet and artist Kenneth Goldsmith, who, in 2015, read Michael Brown's federal autopsy report out loud as a poem at Brown

University's "Interrupt 3" conference. "The Body of Michael Brown" is the lightly altered autopsy report of Michael Brown Jr., a young African American man shot and killed in 2014 by a white police officer named Darren Wilson in Ferguson, Missouri. Goldsmith's project was a continuation of his 2013 book, *Seven American Deaths and Disasters*, titled after Andy Warhol's painting series of the same name, in which Goldsmith reprints the transcripts of seven radio and television reports of national tragedies as they unfolded. *Seven American Deaths and Disasters* is a masterful book, in part because of the tension that arises between what the television and radio personalities witnessed and the constraints of their own media platform. Essentially, the reporters' spontaneous reactions of fear, excitement, horror, shock, and disbelief were contained and curtailed by their understanding that they had to document these feelings in a formal structure that resisted such utterance. *Seven American Deaths* is about the limits of language and representation, and how these limits are institutionally reinforced; it is not primarily about voyeuristic spectacle.

An autopsy report, however, offers no such study in institutional or rhetorical contrasts. The autopsy report has only one language and formal structure in which to work. The coroner is not seeing the shocking event unfold; she is documenting its aftermath. Nothing inside the autopsy report itself is meant to undermine its formal attempts at this scientific task except, perhaps, the coroner. Essentially, there is nothing to read the autopsy report against but the reader's own imagination and understanding of the death itself.

Without that inbuilt tension, that collision of different languages and utterance that might take the gaze away from Michael Brown and turn it back upon the institutions that would depict him, "The Body of Michael Brown" duplicates the gesture of Schutz's

Open Casket: it reduces Michael Brown Jr. to a body to be spectated. Michael Brown transforms into an object of racial fascination in Goldsmith's transcription, a fact that becomes apparent by the end of Goldsmith's version of the report, in which he reportedly finishes the poem with the autopsy's description of Brown's genitals, an attempt to critique the racist fascination with Black male sexuality, which ends up reifying the fascination itself. In that, it mimics the way that Officer Darren Wilson himself later characterized both his own and Brown's bodies, saying that he "felt like a five year-old holding Hulk Hogan" as he attempted to restrain Brown, who looked like a "demon." "The Body of Michael Brown" is a devastatingly apt title for Goldsmith's poem, since that becomes the sole focus of Goldsmith's creative gaze: the limit of Michael Brown's meaning for the White imagination, and the locus of its fear.

This is not to say that, should Schutz or Goldsmith have done something different with their forms, the art would have succeeded. But the artworks fail on the very terms in which they set out to depict their subjects. Their attempts to document Black pain in both instances focus on Black bodily subjectivity without context or resistance. It is a combination of both form and content working not together with but apart from the artist's intentions.

THE LIMITS OF IDENTIFICATION

I don't doubt that Schutz and Goldsmith are, in their personal lives, anti-racist. I also don't doubt that they wanted their art to participate in the critical dismantling of racism. But they each produced work that fits a culturally racist paradigm. Schutz's and Goldsmith's works are different from choosing to adapt the structure and themes of *Journey to the West*, or writing a story in which some of the characters are, say, African American or Chinese or American Indian, characters whose specific presence may be necessary to the story being told, but whose own traumatic cultural memories are not the focus and purpose of the story.

You will note in my discussion of Goldsmith and Schutz that I critique the end result of their creative acts; I don't challenge the right of these artists to have attempted this work. I'm not interested in arguing for or against the right of artists to engage with certain motifs and subjects, largely because I know such an argument can never be definitely answered or policed, and because if the discussion we have around appropriation only becomes an argument to determine what you as a writer are entitled to create, the end result is that we will each be forced to defend deficient positions. I will be arguing against the joy of creativity and the history of art and literature, you will fall back on outdated arguments around "universal human experience" that make you appear willfully insensitive to the effects of bodily difference in our world.

As a writer and a teacher, and most especially as a mixed-race woman, I don't believe that writing outside one's subject position is always and only a culturally appropriative act. Because to insist that a writer must be from the same group identity as the voice of the author has a dangerous flip side to it: while it warns off writers from blithely taking on subject matters outside their own experience, it also implicitly warns writers within the same group identity that an authentic experience of that identity *does* exist—to the group at least—and can and may be policed from within.

But as I write this to you, X, it also strikes me that, implicit in this discussion of creative rights is a deeper anxiety around reading itself. Is literature populated with characters I was *not* meant to identify with? How much of my reading was supposed to reflect my specific sense of self, my own experience in the world? Have I ever seen myself—fully—on the page? The answer is no, ironically, even when I have written that depiction *of* myself on the page. Something about me is always missing, certain qualities and emotions elevated, others suppressed. Have you ever seen yourself in your entirety in a story or a novel? I doubt it. And I think you know most literary characters are, even when complexly detailed, still sketches of humanity that resemble but never duplicate us. A sensitive reader understands she is different from the character that she reads, and it is perhaps because of that difference she is able and willing to inhabit more aspects of that character. As a reader I am refracted by, not always reflected in, language. Reading does not demand total and exact duplication of my identity in order for me to feel, otherwise I couldn't enjoy literature at all.

But I'm also aware these refractions have amplified certain metaphorical meanings around our identities, and that these meanings can also be harmful. Writers and theorists from James Baldwin to Claudia Rankine have argued that the human imagination is shaped by our experience in the world, and these experiences have become linked to social, aesthetic, and political conceptions of our bodily differences. Toni Morrison, in her critical book *Playing in the Dark: Whiteness and the Literary Imagination*, reminds us that depictions of race in literature in particular have become a way "of referring to and disguising forces, events, classes and expressions of social decay and economic division." Racial difference takes on social meanings that are proliferated through stereotypes and preserved as widely held beliefs. Here are just a few of the personal traits you and I are trained to assign racial meaning to: intelligence, sexuality, physical and artistic talent, aesthetic preferences, financial prowess. Racial meanings have been historically constructed and institutionally reinforced; these meanings do not appear overnight but become intricately coded through government legislation, religious dogma, and artistic representations.

When non-White bodies are changed into symbolic vehicles to conceptualize larger social forces and ideals, I have to be aware that these amplifications reflect long-held systems of literary and political power that privilege the White writer's imagination and position in the world. In that, the issue of appropriation is never just a personal decision to write about what and whom I want to. While we each strive to live and create independently, we are also connected to one another by community and history. We are never the free individuals that we imagine we are.

UNDERSTANDING THE COMPLEXITIES OF RACE AND IDENTITY

At heart, the risk with turning race into a metaphor is that it can essentialize racial identity. It suggests there must be something authentic and unchangeable about our bodily differences, an argument that has been—ironically—shared by both segregationists and racial progressives alike when they demand we each "stay in our lanes," a phrase I find particularly bemusing, because as a third-generation Asian American woman who is racially half-Chinese and half-White, where exactly am I supposed to drive? Perhaps I can choose to categorize myself as Asian American, or as Chinese American or both, but I might also choose to see myself as mixed-race.

Perhaps, based on my White-reading appearance to certain observers, I might identify myself culturally only as White. But why should I identify myself according to other people's perceptions? And if I do categorize myself as mixed-race, what could possibly constitute a mixed-race *culture* outside of my appearance, itself hardly shared with other mixed-race people? Do I have any claim, outside of the difference of my physical appearance, to a Chinese cultural identity, especially as I do not speak the language, rarely cook Chinese food at home, do not live in an enclave with other Chinese-descended people, and am only mildly inconvenienced by my family's watered-down Confucian values? At the same time, regardless of my paternal family lineage, can I believably claim to be any part Norwegian? And what exactly is "Norwegian" supposed to mean, when I was born and raised in America?

If culture is defined as a group that possesses a distinct set of physical features, a specific language, religious practice, or food, arts, and music, and that is bound by geography or the same set of moral, political, familial, or ethical values, you can see how much variation and even contradiction exist inside what you and I might offhandedly treat as a monolithic group, such as African Americans or LGBTQI people. Even highly specific group identities, such as Navajo or Pakistani, which might at first seem more clearly bounded by a set of shared values and customs, quickly become more complex constructions, as these cultures, too, do not live in isolation. Like any other cultural group, they change over time, and of course they come into contact with people from all over the world through marriage, migration, adoption, and assimilation.

Obviously one of the reasons I've found my lane difficult to navigate is that my racial identity is not my cultural one. The terms "culture" and "race" intersect in our imagination, since these terms have been interchangeably used and often conflated. It's largely understood by biologists that race is a social construct that groups people together based on the similarity of physical appearance and features, while ethnicity refers to one's cultural affiliation. Occasionally, race and ethnicity share some connection, as with Chinese Americans who also choose to consider themselves Asian American. But sometimes race and ethnicity are different, as when a Black woman born in Italy identifies herself as Italian, and also Black. You can be many different ethnicities at once—Mormon, American, and Navajo, say—but it's harder for people to accept that you can be multiply raced. This is because racial definitions are imposed on us due to appearance, while ethnicity can be based on personal choice. You can learn a different language, convert to a religion, eat different foods. But you can't, unless you're Rachel Dolezal, suddenly claim to be Black. Ethnic identity may be both internally and externally constructed, too, as in the example of Latinx or Hispanic Americans, who may be seen as comprising a single monolithic cultural group defined by their appearance, but who quickly identify themselves according to even more specific cultural groups, such as Mexican Americans, or Colombian Americans, or Cuban Americans. And, of course, these cultures break down further, based on indigeneity, geographical affiliation, migration, and language.

The difference between race and ethnicity is something that's explored in Jhumpa Lahiri's short story "When Mr. Pirzada Came to Dine," in which Mr. Pirzada, a Bengali-Muslim man and visiting academic to Boston, is temporarily befriended by another academic Indian family living in Boston during the Indo-Pakistan war of 1971. Lilia, the young Indian American narrator of the story who was born and raised in the States, calls Mr. Pirzada "the Indian man," even though her father explains he is Muslim and Pakistani. Lilia can't understand this: they eat the same food, speak the same language; they certainly look the same. And in fact, it is in part based on this shared racial appearance that Mr. Pirzada has been adopted by Lilia's family at all, since her mother, missing her birth country, calls up and invites to dinner any stranger with an Indian-sounding name she finds in the university directory. In India, Mr. Pirzada would remain a Muslim stranger to Lilia's family; in America, his racial difference from White Americans makes him a friend, allowing for a kind of cross-ethnic connection that might not happen in their home country.

We all rely on the shorthand of racial and cultural identity even as we also recognize the limitations of this way of thinking about ourselves. That said, while our identities are fluid, some part of cultural belonging can always be definitively answered, through citizenship or clan and tribal membership records. But outside of this historical record-keeping, the question of who we are remains tantalizingly out of bounds. Though cultures are defined by shared beliefs and traits, once I find someone who possesses the traits I define as essential to her culture, I will just as quickly find someone within that culture who defies or lacks those same traits and abilities. And as cultures change over time, I have to change my ideas about what should comprise these traits and abilities. That's why, as you might recall, so many people were offended by Elizabeth Warren's DNA test to determine whether she was Cherokee. Culture isn't in the blood, it's performed, and with American Indians, it's also about being tribally claimed. To insist that DNA gives us our identity is both fetishistic and essentialist. If every culture had a universally approved "essence," then writing outside my subject position would be easy because I could know the limits of their representation. *This* is what it means to be Tlingkit. *That* is what it means to be Guyanese.

I bring all this up, X, to point out how much you might be overlooking in our discussion of cultural appropriation if you and I simply treat this as a questionable artistic practice. I want to trouble any assumptions you might have about race and culture, which includes the belief that culture and race are tied to specific, easily categorized and immutable identities that can be performed on the page through the use of symbols or virtue signaling.

Maybe you already know that, but if you and I know race is not something that can be essentialized, then why have we turned race into such a powerful metaphor in our literature? The answer to that lies deep in the Enlightenment, when, starting in 1735, Carl Linnaeus created human racial hierarchies in his *Systema Naturae*, attaching specific characteristics to races he termed White, Yellow, Red, and Black. Linnaeus's taxonomy served as the backbone of Europe's social coding and imagination of race, in which race became what the scholar Henry Louis Gates Jr. calls "a trope of ultimate, irreducible difference between cultures, linguistic groups, or adherents of specific belief systems . . . Race [became] the ultimate trope of difference because it [was] so very arbitrary in its difference." Ironically, because race can't biologically uphold or explain differences in our innate characteristics, racism must be supported by increasingly subjective rules of difference, including what Gates calls a careless use of language that we deploy to maintain those differences. It's this careless figurative language that has essentially "willed" or reified natural differences between people into formulaic ones.

Here's an example of what I'm talking about: Katy Perry, dressed as a geisha, performing her hit song "Unconditionally" for the 2013 American Musical Awards.

If you've seen the performance, you'll remember that Perry was dressed as a geisha in pink and white, her stage filled with cherry-blossom branches, red lacquer bridges, taiko drummers, and black-haired girls all dressed in yukata while twirling paper fans. The only thing missing was Scarlett Johansson dressed as Hello Kitty practicing karate in a corner.

The problem with this performance wasn't that Perry took material objects from Japan as stage props, but that her performance invested these objects with racial difference itself. Katy Perry's decision to dress as a geisha while singing a song about loving someone "unconditionally" linked Japanese characteristics and culture with unalterable devotion, an Orientalist trope of the submissive Asian female that's existed since the late nineteenth century, due to the popularity of the 1898 short story "Madame Butterfly" by John Luther Long (itself an adaptation of the 1887 French novel *Madame Chrysanthème* by Pierre Loti) and the Puccini opera it inspired, *Madama Butterfly*. Perry's appropriation (of an appropriation of an appropriation) darken the meaning of "Unconditionally," a song whose lyrics declare only that the singer will adore her lover regardless of his insecurities. Her costume and stage visuals were meant to evoke the end of *Madama Butterfly*, in which Cio-Cio San kills herself after discovering her American lover has been faithless.

If Perry had been singing another song entirely and worn a kimono, that would have been appropriative but it wouldn't have crossed the line into racism. Her performance and Japanese clothing visually argued that the most effective way of proving her undying devotion to a lover was by displaying herself as a Japanese woman. Because that's how Asian women love.

And that, X, is a perfect example of harmful cultural appropriation.

Essentially, works that engage in cultural appropriation traffic in stereotypes that link bodily and cultural difference with innate physical and mental characteristics. They are works that ask us not just to perceive a character's racial difference but to see how those external characteristics *stand in metaphorically* for more profound interior difference. Artistic appropriation itself does not require that the artist reflect racist values, but oftentimes, appropriation occurs *because* the artist's ideas of people of color are racist.

Here you're probably thinking that the issue of cultural appropriation has been neatly solved. Write about people outside your subject position all you want, just don't stereotype them. Of course, this is easier said than done. Much of writing a character well is based on imagining *extremely* specific details about his or her background. It's not enough to consider how someone's African American racial appearance affects her identity according to our general knowledge about African Americans; you also have to consider her education, her environment, her class, her family's history, and her religious background. Basically, you aren't just writing about and through racial appearance, you are writing about how people assert themselves as individuals within their own racial and ethnic constructions.

On top of that, even though we understand that racial and cultural identities depend at times on fantasies, we still also recognize that the ways we read race and culture have real consequences and are also based on recognizable differences. Cultures can change and still be distinct from one another; globalization may have put more of us into contact with one another's values and products, but it has not made all of us the same. So while fantasies of authenticity certainly shape identity, there are also real, shared experiences that connect individuals within a group with one another, and with the art they themselves produce.

This is something the writer and musician Amiri Baraka and the jazz musician Charlie Parker both believed was at the heart of Black art. Baraka even argued a musician couldn't learn to play the blues well except through what he called "the peculiar social, cultural, economic and emotional experience of a Black man in America." As he saw it, "The idea of a white blues singer seems an even more violent contradiction of terms than the idea of a middle-class blues singer. The materials of the blues [are] not available to the white American." Parker, more pithily, expressed it this way: "If you don't live it, it won't come out of your horn."

Maybe you're struck by Baraka's statement that Whiteness, for a blues singer, would make for an even more "violent contradiction" than being middle class, largely because this argument would also imply, at some level, an exact duplication of all parts of the "authentic" blues musician's identity. So can a middle-class, Harvard-educated African American *woman* who's never been a sharecropper become an "authentic" blues guitarist? Can someone Latinx? How is anyone supposed to reconcile the problem, say, of Eric Clapton?

Sadly, there is no unbreakable link between one's identity and one's success as an artist representing particular cultural art forms or experiences. When it comes to aesthetics and cultural appropriation, then, what we're talking about at some point is the desire to locate the single and unchangeable characteristic, trait, belief, or behavior that all members of a particular group must possess. To possess this particular essence would suggest the possessor be able to enter into that culture and perform the stories and arts of that identity fluidly.

That's why determining what constitutes a stereotype becomes so tricky, X: I recognize that I can't invest racial difference with particular meanings at the same time I know that racial difference shapes our experience of the world into legible patterns. With regard to writing and appropriation, the real question is not whether I can simply ignore or override racial stereotypes, or even whether certain cultures have immutable claims to particular subjects and content, but what appetites I feed when I write from a position outside of my own.

REFRAMING THE QUESTION OF APPROPRIATION

If we reframe the discussion of cultural appropriation around the question of appetites, I believe we'll move the conversation to a more productive place, one that allows writers like you and me a way to better evaluate appropriative work, and to understand how our own racial thinking has been shaped. This is part of what Claudia Rankine and Beth Loffreda, in their introduction to the anthology *The Racial Imaginary: Writers on Race in the Life of the Mind*, want to do in their deconstruction of what they call "the racial imaginary": a space in which "the boundaries of one's imaginative sympathy line up, again and again, with the lines drawn by power." In essence, once we write into and about race, we are pulled by profound feelings that have framed how we are taught to see race. If White writers in particular don't question this emotional framing of both racial and cultural meaning, they risk duplicating the institutional language and thinking that privileges its own power at the expense of people of color.

The solution, Loffreda and Rankine suggest, is not "to extend the imagination into other identities" on the page, but to imagine new ways in which a writer's work could

> expose that racial dynamic . . . not imaginatively inhabit the other because that is their right as artists, but instead embody and examine the interior landscape that wishes to speak of rights, that wishes to move freely and unbounded across time, space and lines of power, that wishes to inhabit whomever it chooses.

Loffreda and Rankine don't deny the possibility of writing in the voice of a character of color, only that the writer's imagination should give her certain "rights" as an artist to claim this voice. As I wrote before, our imaginations are limited and earthbound, something even my abbreviated description of race and ethnic theory should suggest. When it comes to addressing the ethical problems of appropriative writing, Loffreda and Rankine argue that you and I must ask cannier questions about its purpose. Rather than wondering, "Can I write from another's point of view . . . instead: to ask why and what for, not just if and how?" Loffreda and Rankine want us to consider appropriation "not in terms of prohibition and rights, but desire."

"Desire" is a fascinating word to use in this context, and I don't think it should be read as an urge that excuses any form of appropriation. Just because I feel pulled to write outside my subject position doesn't mean that my desire authenticates the act. I can make bad decisions out of desire as well as good ones, and perhaps I might end up perpetuating a stereotype because some unexamined part of me cannot bear to abandon it.

Like Loffreda and Rankine, I, too, see appropriation finally as a question of desire, and I want to press upon the ways in which our ideas about aesthetic "rights," creative practices, and the publishing industry itself might be racially framed and segregated. Like Loffreda and Rankine, I believe that asking *why* and *what for* deepens the conversation, because these questions also ask whether the presence of certain voices helps unfold a more ethically imagined story. If one were to write, say, about slavery in the United States and not have an African American character in the novel, certainly that absence—even if meant sensitively—would be both wounding and absurd. Unlike Loffreda and Rankine, however, I think it's important to examine the *ifs* and *hows* of writing in the voice of characters of color, because I do believe that models exist to study, and that studying them might expand our knowledge of how our imagination around race and identity gets shaped, and perpetuated through our writing.

THE PROBLEMS OF EMPATHY

Before I end this letter, I want to unknit the term "desire" that Loffreda and Rankine use, which to me suggests the writer's solipsism but also her compulsion to empathize with people unlike herself. It signals a passionate attachment to, if not always the complete comprehension of, her characters, and in that sense might also indicate the fidelity she feels to her vision of how identities function in the world. And while I, as a teacher, praise empathy as a fundamental classroom value when it comes to discussion, as a writer, I'm suspicious of empathy as a critical or creative value. "Empathy" is a word that shows up in our common English lexicon in 1904, around the same time that the nickelodeon and cinema were developing. I don't think this is a coincidence. Mass media and public spectacle allowed people to see the world through other characters' perspectives. They encouraged us to be moved by stories as a group, as part of a group experience. These were visual narratives that manipulated audience response through sound, story, and astonishing images. They were also stories about people who didn't exist. All of which is to say that, as a writer, I'm aware that a mediated representation of people unlike me can help me see from another perspective, while I also understand that through reading, I become *empathetic to a portrayal* of an identity, versus connected to an actual person.

Of course, I can hear your rejoinder: Isn't that the same thing? To empathize with someone's story still brings me into closer contact with anyone who has experienced that story, whether or not she "only" exists in fiction. My point, however, is that writers manipulate language to get the emotional effects we want and that, having gotten those effects, these emotions can stand in for the harder task of working for social change.

I'm also suspicious of elevating readerly empathy to a literary value because, in this regard, there is a tendency to treat empathy as a precursor to color-blindness. If all of us finally behave and feel and think in similar ways, how much can race—and specifically being raced as non-White—really matter? This argument suggests that bodily and cultural difference might be something we should finally ignore, perhaps becoming something akin to flaws in the "post-racial" society that should be brushed aside by focusing on "what links us all together," meaning that writing will ultimately be coded for majority readers by focusing on events, experiences, and emotions that do not particularly challenge them.

Likewise, when we treat the stories of White people as "universal," do we then understand our reading about the interior lives of White characters as an act of empathy, or a reflection of our own humanity? Is it, say, an act of empathy only when a White person reads about people of color, since people of color are trained to take the White character's viewpoint as a default position?

I believe that empathy activates and preserves communal memory, X; it extends the historical record by asking people to carry the narratives of others not like them in their own mind, and that is no small thing. Empathy allows us to transcend the damaging effects of historical institutions such as slavery or genocide by paying witness to them, by intimately imagining and understanding their construction and effects. And yet readers should be mindful of the artifice and racial hierarchies built into the creation of any empathetic performance. Empathy may be a profound, exciting, and beneficial emotion, but it cannot be used to justify or critically frame any work engaged in appropriation. As the writer Namwali Serpell suggests in her article "The Banality of Empathy," perhaps you and I might employ Hannah Arendt's theory of "representative thinking" instead of empathy in our writing, which means that rather than trying to imaginatively *become* another person in our work, you and I imagine our own thoughts and feelings but from another person's position. "Representative thinking" is akin to what Loffreda and Rankine argue for in *The Racial Imaginary*, when our imagination encourages us to visit but not encompass or homogenize the other's perspective. By doing this, you and I maintain our own detachment while also respecting the independence of the other person's experience.

There's one final note I'd like to add about empathy as a possible definition of desire. I find it bemusing that when we talk about empathetic forms of appropriation, we often speculate about how to write about the trauma of a marginalized community. However, one obvious but little practiced way to write about the trauma of racism, say, would be for a White writer to imagine the position of the racist. Why not write about slavery from the slaver's perspective? Remarkably few writers have done this, perhaps because it is more appealing to imagine yourself as the victim rather than the perpetrator of violence, perhaps because the White writer fears that the audience would do to her what it tends to do to the writer of color, which is to collapse the identity of the narrator with that of the author. Regardless, the story of racism does not simply happen to people of color. In a White-centered society, racism necessitates the presence of White people, and so the White writer could easily empathize with a multitude of historical traumas by locating her Whiteness as the subject to be examined.

For me, as a writer, one of the most dangerous side effects of empathetic desire when it appropriates another culture's trauma is that it conflates the underrepresented community with its marginalization and pain. These in turn risk becoming the community's authenticating narratives, both for readers outside and within the community. Because if writers outside a marginalized community imagine its trauma poorly, writers from within the community will be spurred to respond, to correct the record. Their artistic resistance becomes, over time, a feedback loop. If the literary marketplace publishes stories appropriated on the basis of their empathetic reception, we risk letting the narrative of racism and trauma for writers of color prevail, because that's what the literary system recognizes as authentic based on its publishing record, and that's also what the writer of color can ensure is distinctly within her autobiographical control. Over time, the literary marketplace and the writer of color unconsciously but complicitly work to fuse the raced identity with pain, with suffering, with racism, with psychic damage. This system of literary power requires that writers, in trying to dismantle the system, are implicitly put in a position of performing their own disempowerment for an audience eager to understand it, thus this disenfranchisement becomes the primary trope that both the publishing world and the writer of color can agree frames the writer of color's experience as different from the White writer's.

And I think this, again, is why it's offensive to many writers to see the experience of racism appropriated. Not only is this an experience we suspect the White writer hasn't had, it also reifies something few of us want to imagine: I am the body that is wounded, othered, stigmatized. It makes racial difference a continuing trauma that must only be endured, never celebrated. And I don't think that's how most people of color experience their bodies, or the world.

When it comes to the question of desire, respect, and appropriation in your own writing, X, perhaps you might ask yourself the following questions:

- Whose desire animates your text?
- In what ways does this desire replicate hierarchies and stories you are already familiar with?
- Does this desire expand or contract historical memory, and in what ways does this desire encourage you to investigate you own racial meaning?
- Is your understanding of your own identity at the margin or the center of the story?
- Does your identity *need* to be at the margin or the center of this story?

This last question is particularly important to consider, because if you overlay your own interior reality onto the lives of other people, you grant them the humanity that you have. While this might sound appealing, how then does this desire overlook the humanity that *your characters* have? In other words, in what ways does your desire free your characters, and in what ways does it continue to constrain them?

Finally, X, in what ways does your desire let you imagine, and create, joy?

LETTER THREE

Truth, Accuracy, and the
Commodification of Identity

Dear X:

Several months ago, a poem published in *The Nation* kicked up a controversy on social media and in journals around the country. The poem was entitled "How-To," and it's by Anders Carlson-Wee. If you haven't read it, here's the poem in its entirety:

> If you got hiv, say aids. If you a girl,
> say you're pregnant––nobody gonna lower
> themselves to listen for the kick. People
> passing fast. Splay your legs, cock a knee
> funny. It's the littlest shames they're likely
> to comprehend. Don't say homeless, they know
> you is. What they don't know is what opens
> a wallet, what stops em from counting

what they drop. If you're young say younger.
Old say older. If you're crippled don't
flaunt it. Let em think they're good enough
Christians to notice. Don't say you pray,
say you sin. It's about who they believe
they is. You hardly even there.

"How-To" attracted a lot of attention after a number of online readers wrote that they found the poem culturally appropriative, in part
because they knew that Carlson-Wee himself is not homeless but educated, White, and middle class; in part because of the poem's use of
racial, or perhaps regional, dialect. Was the speaker African American? From the South? Poor? A woman? A man? A combination of these
identities? Admirers of the poem defended the use of dialect, arguing
that not only did the poem sound like people they knew from their own
states and families, but that it exactly duplicated the dialectical rules of
Appalachian English. I myself am not an expert on this dialect, and so
the controversy made me wonder whether it was possible that a speaker's voice can be both accurate and inauthentic-sounding at once to
readers, and how much readerly fantasies of how people should sound
play into our reception of what we call a character's "voice." Reading
"How-To" now, I find myself turning to Loffreda and Rankine's question: What particular desires are on display in the poem?

    If I rewrite Carlson-Wee's poem in standardized English, I see
that the meaning of the poem doesn't change. To survive on the
streets, the homeless person reinvents himself to activate each passerby's particular sense of empathy and guilt. This is a message I find
believable as a reader. If this poem were spoken by an African American, however, I might imagine some crucial bit of information was

still missing, which is that—for some passersby—there is no performance that can activate empathy, because it won't see or respond to
Black poverty. If it's true that people give based on "who they believe
/ they is," then certain White or non-Black passersby will only give
money to Whites. Or, conversely, they'll offer more money to non-
White homeless people so as not to appear racist.

I recognize how particular identities might affect homelessness.
Being a woman would affect one's experience of being homeless.
Being disabled, being a vet, being mentally ill, being non-White:
all these identities would profoundly shape how one survived on
the streets. But the poem suggests that all identity positions might
be leveled through performance to appeal to a passerby's desire to
see herself—or her idea of homelessness—reflected in the speaker.
Interestingly, the poem itself refers to categories of identities that
are, for moments of time at least, unseen or hard to immediately
confirm: "If you got hiv, say aids," the speaker suggests, just as he
also suggests a homeless person might claim to be younger than her
age or, if a woman, pregnant. And yet the practical experience of
being embodied means that certain performances are finally either
limited or impossible to act out by the actual fact of our bodies.

Likewise, if the poem's meaning suggests that identity is ultimately a filigree, a mask that can be put on and taken off at will, the
dialect itself insists upon the opposite message, which is that behind
the mask lies a highly specific identity; the dialect may even imply
a historical or geographic reason for the speaker's homelessness.
Thus the poem, which attempts to impart a general message about
a wide variety of identity positions experiencing homelessness, now
also tries to act as an individual dramatic monologue, one spoken by
someone who, through his or her dialectical tics, represents a par-

ticular community and sweep of history. In that, the poem requires me to envision who the speaker is, not just to see through his or her perspective. If I can't easily name or even physically imagine the narrator, the poem becomes the performance of a didactic message, not a fully fleshed character study.

I think this is why Carlson-Wee's use of dialect, regardless of its accuracy, risked feeling primarily performative to readers, not merely a mark of identity difference from the author himself, but potentially of identity *otherness*. In some sense, the poem's use of dialect unconsciously mimics the speaker's own message: it performs my idea of the person who is homeless, versus trying to carve out an identity specific to a person. Identity otherness is what "How-To" accidentally achieves, because the exact racial or regional identity of the poem's speaker gives its readers no more complicated a sense of how visibility might be socially coded, enforced, or personally experienced.

But while I question the use of dialect in "How-To," I wouldn't argue against using dialect or Black English in another work. I certainly wouldn't argue against Carlson-Wee's impulse to consider the connection between speech and character in a poem that wants to investigate social performance. The playwright and actress Anna Deavere Smith, famous for her documentary-style plays in which she performs a variety of ethnically diverse characters, says that voice itself is a profound physical reality; how we speak is not a cultural tic, she says in her introduction to *Fires in the Mirror*, but something that involves all our bodily knowledge. Speech patterns are crucial to signaling ethnic affiliation and background. Our identities are shaped in and by language, and so it makes sense to have people sound like the communities from which they come. My point with "How-To" is that we have no clear idea *how* the speaker's particular voice matters in the poem outside of triggering the reader's potential voyeurism. With regard to Loffreda and Rankine's question about desire, there is no "why" given other than Carlson-Wee's desire to portray his speaker as somehow unlike the author.

When I followed the poem's progress online, I noticed a number of critics argued that the poem's dialectical inaccuracy was a sign Carlson-Wee didn't respect or understand the people he'd portrayed. Considering the poem's underlying liberal message, I suspect Carlson-Wee has a great desire to signal his respect for homeless people. Still, I want to spend a little time thinking about the problems of using accuracy as the primary standard for respectful appropriation. One of the difficulties about accuracy is that sometimes it runs distinctly parallel or even counter to truth, and when it comes to dialect, exact duplication can have the opposite effect of the one you intend as a writer, which is to make your characters sound like cartoons. Truth, which is the writer's aim, can at times differ from factual "accuracy," but part of how we recognize something as true is that it has a strong relationship *with* accuracy. We approximate how people speak in order to elevate what we want the reader to focus on: how they behave and think and feel.

Accuracy, in terms of speech, focuses on bodily rhythm, what you might call the twang and rasp of speech. These things, if attended to closely by the writer, allow a reader to feel the physical complexity of a person's speech patterns, even while they may also miss the truth of the person's actual *voice*, that internal monologue—or perhaps dialogue—that comprises the self. Voice differs from speech by the fact it is composed of a ceaseless stream of impressions formed through memory, sense, and emotion, all of which trigger more memories and emotions as we internally narrate the story of our lives. This inner voice may be outside of language, or at least outside any conventional syntax you and I have been taught. And because our inner voices move so associatively, representing them on the page is, frankly, impossible: as a writer, I depict a character's inner voice through outline, by focusing not just on how she says a thing, but on what she says, and the order in which she says it. In that sense, my representation of speech sacrifices exactitude to locate a more radical truth.

Writing manipulates details to create worlds that readers choose to see as believable because they reflect what readers already know or assume to know about a person or event. One of my friends, Jennifer Sinor, wrote a work of lyric nonfiction reimagining the life of Georgia O'Keeffe entitled, *Letters Like the Day: On Reading Georgia O'Keeffe,* in which she includes a short scene of Georgia O'Keeffe snorkeling. Did O'Keeffe ever go snorkeling? Jennifer has no idea. The scene was written to give the literary character O'Keeffe a moment to visualize the underwater world in shapes and light and color that recall the way O'Keeffe will later paint the New Mexican landscape. It's a completely invented scene, but it feels organic because of what we know about O'Keeffe's paintings. In my own personal essays, I change the order in which certain events happen for narrative clarity, and because I don't have perfect recollection of everything that's been said to me since I was five years old, I occasionally create dialogue that replicates what a person I know very well could have said.

Percy Bysshe Shelley, in *A Defence of Poetry,* wrote that poetry is the art of "imagining that which we know." In essence, writers lie or imagine at times to get the larger story right. And these small manipulations are, ironically, part of what makes fictional narratives feel truthful to readers, even as they frustrate accuracy. But these manipulations I cite are small examples of fakery that risk very little damage. Our historical reading of Georgia O'Keeffe does not depend on knowing whether she went snorkeling. Likewise, no one in or outside my family cares whether my great-aunt Ruby hated orange sherbet. But my family does know how religious Ruby was, and so it would be offensive to them, not just inaccurate, for me to make her suddenly burst into a sacrilegious screed. Creative non-fiction and poetry make no claims to be journalism, which *must* depend upon accuracy and fact to be both believable and truthful. But when it comes to creatively imagining the lives of people unlike us, certain inventions take on larger ethical resonances. I don't doubt that Carlson-Wee spent time with homeless people, that he likely even heard a homeless person say something like "How-To" to him. I don't think, however, that he pressed as hard as he could into the complexities of this truth about homelessness that he'd witnessed.

I also don't fault Carlson-Wee's poem on the basis of his own identity position. I don't assume that because he is educated or White, able-bodied or middle-class, he couldn't possibly write a good poem about homelessness. As I wrote before, it's the essential absence of meaning to the speaker's performed identity in the poem that I question, its lack of any central *what for* and *why*.

ACCURACY, ETHICS, AND IDEALISM

While the debate around Carlson-Wee's poem raises questions about truth versus accuracy, you should know this particular debate has raged before—and far more hotly—after William Styron's 1967 novel, *The Confessions of Nat Turner*, was published. The title of Styron's Pulitzer Prize–winning novel comes from Turner's oral history transcribed by the White lawyer T. R. Gray, a notorious racist whose own problematic editing of the text have led historians to question the accuracy of Gray's transcription. But while Gray's transcript shapes the basis for Turner's language rhythms in the novel, it doesn't form Styron's own imagination of Turner's character. In Styron's *Confessions*, Turner is far more conflicted about how he feels about the other slaves he wants to free, as well as about his own actions in the rebellion he led. Styron also changed some basic facts of Turner's life, stating that Turner was taught to read by a paternalistic White slave owner rather than by his parents, and that Turner was celibate, though in real life he was married.

It's these narrative changes around Turner's sexual life that I think present the novel's starkest problems. In the novel, Turner engages in a homosexual act with a younger slave named Wills, who attends Turner's spiritual conversion, an event Styron imagines having occurred in Turner's youth. He also includes two extremely graphic rape fantasies that Turner has of different White women, one being Margaret Whitehead, a plantation owner's religious daughter whom Turner later kills. Whitehead and the other White female characters come to represent all the ways in which Turner—as a Black man—is emasculated by slavery. In Styron's novel, Turner kills only Whitehead in his rebellion, a murder that conflates Turner's misogyny with his desire to recover his sense of masculinity, and his spiritual calling to destroy slavery.

It's this obsessive triangulation between Turner's sexuality, his misogyny, and his commitment to rebellion that gives me pause. In the novel, women provide Turner the greatest temptation both to unleash racial violence and also to prevent it. When Turner stumbles across a weeping White woman, her naked expression of grief unleashes in him a violent response in which he writes:

> I [began] to possess her without tenderness . . . but with abrupt,
> brutal, and rampaging fury . . . [M]y black hands already tear-
> ing at the lustrous billowing silk as I drew the dress up around
> her waist, and forcing apart those soft white thighs.

The rape fantasy continues for almost a page, and this is the least explicit language I can excerpt from it. The fantasy ends with a description of the woman crying out in orgasm, a scene that distantly corresponds to the rape fantasy Turner later has of Whitehead, a young woman who alternates in the novel between appearing devout, sexually knowing, and bizarrely naïve. In one scene, she trips into the plantation's library wearing only pantalettes, startling Turner, who muses on the "glimpse of the dim shadowed cleft between the round promontories where [the] fabric [clung] tightly to her firm young bot-tom." "[H]ad I not been a Negro and therefore presumably unstirred by such a revealing sight," Turner thinks bitterly to himself, "she would never be so immodest to flaunt thus beneath my nose . . . How could she with this thoughtlessness and innocence provoke me so? Godless white bitch."

Prior to his decision to lead the slave rebellion, however, Turner balks, imagining instead "spend[ing] upon [Margaret] all afternoon a backed-up lifetime of passion" that might allow him to "forget [his] great mission."

Styron portrays Turner as morally ambiguous, which is under-standable, given that the righteous are brain-numbing to encoun-ter, in life or on the page. But as the novel unfolds, Turner's attitudes toward other slaves as well as his attraction to Whitehead becomes less ambiguous than an opportunity for Styron to depict Turner according to stereotypical tropes. In one scene, Turner observes his fellow slaves asleep in a wagon on their way to a market to be sold, and rather than being moved by their situation, Turner notes instead how:

> [s]lumbrous in broad daylight, they would flop asleep against the side boards of the wagon, pink lips wet and apart . . . Like animals they relinquished the past with as much dumb composure as they accepted the present, and were unaware of any future at all. Such creatures deserve to be sold, I thought bitterly, and I was torn between devastation for them and regret that it was too late for me to save them through the power of the Word.

Of course, enslaved in a racist system, it makes sense that Turner would be infected by the language that surrounds him, but the novel relies too often on Turner's objectification of other Black people, criticizing them in the language of his enslavers, with little critique of this language on his part. The novel is largely absent of Black women, too, though it is populated by Black men who appear on the page more as references than people; many are passing acquaintances who share brief colloquies with Turner, disappearing after only a few paragraphs. Hunt, Hark, and Wills, the most prominent Black characters beside Turner, share a limited part of the novel's action. Their subordination as characters, along with the fact that many of the other African Americans are often depicted as passive animals, reinforces Turner's assessment of his fellow slaves: they are moony followers, not people he might love and save.

But these problems, notable as they are, take second place to the ways in which Styron depicts gender in the novel. Styron argued in *The Nation* that he created Margaret Whitehead specifically to give Turner some sense of humanity, as well as to suggest this relationship was quintessential to Black-White relations. Turner's fanta-sies about Whitehead, Styron wrote, while factually insupportable, were plausible: the stereotype of "the black man's hang-up on white females," he wrote, was not itself inherently racist but a reflection of how Turner may have been driven by "unspeakable hang-ups and desires." Meanwhile, Turner's imagined celibacy was itself meant to be a metaphor for the "puritanical" and "ascetic" nature of Turner's revolutionary spirit.

About Whitehead as a character, Styron, in an interview recorded for *Per/Se* in 1966, said that he imagined her as "an eighteen-year-old nubile, religious nut . . . unconsciously flirtatious . . . a little dish, a little sweetheart, you know?" This is, generally, how she comes across in the novel. And in this, she joins Styron's parade of flirts and actual whores. Even Turner's mother is portrayed as sexually suspect, a woman who, when held at knifepoint by a White overseer who rapes her in the kitchen, appears to enjoy her rape.

Rape plays a large part in Turner's novel, and even if most of it is only imagined, Styron's depictions of Turner's fantasies link his spir-itual commitment and rebellion with sex. When mutual masturba-tion marks Turner's spiritual conversion, and rape fantasies shadow his decision about whether or not to rebel, then his celibacy—a fac-tual inaccuracy—takes on enormous ethical implications in Styron's depiction of him, because it delegitimizes Turner's uprising, turning it from a moral campaign to a series of Freudian grudges.

Styron's understanding of Turner was filtered through what he termed "a plausible imagination" of history. But you can see that plausibility is conflated here with Styron's own imagination of Black male sexuality, with its "hang-ups" on White women, as well as on misogynist caricatures. The consistent portrayal of Turner as sexually aberrant creates a character whose moral complexity and personal commitment to anti-racist revolution depends on a common White male fear of and fascination with Black men, something, interestingly, that's repeated by one of Turner's owners, a Reverend Epps, who grabs Turner's inner thigh one day and says, "I hear tell a nigger boy's got an unusual big pecker on him. That right, boy?" In such moments, *The Confessions of Nat Turner* is not interested in making a character believable to *all* audiences: it is an appeal to the White male imagination of both Black men and Southern women, and uses sexist and racist tropes to appeal to this particular concept of history.

But while the literary depiction of Turner may be demeaning to Turner's factual legacy, you could also argue that the loudest criticism against Styron's novel was that it didn't fit conceptions of Turner that American audiences wanted at the time. Published in 1967 during the rising Black Power movement, a period in which Martin Luther King's popularity among African Americans was also in decline, Styron's Turner neither fulfilled White Americans' longing for a pacifist Black savior, nor did it appeal to those in the Black Power movement, for whom Turner was a revolutionary hero whose uprising could be read as a contemporary parable for U.S. race relations.

All of which is to say, X, that our ideas about what constitutes "accuracy" might be historically contextualized and approved as much as fabricated. As you know, some part of a work's critical reception is outside the writer's control, and part of believability is based upon the *reader's* desires and presuppositions: beliefs the writer has to challenge as much as she plays with them. Reading *The Confessions of Nat Turner* almost sixty years after it was published, I can see how Styron's characterization of Turner is limited by stereotypes, but I see too that I might fail Styron, if I demand that the book only give me characters I can identify with according to my own idealism. By insisting that literary characters conform to political virtues that exactly duplicate my own, I risk misreading a text according to its reflection of my own historical moment.

Clearly, this is what I'm doing when I critique Turner's relationships with women, but as I argued before with "Effort at Speech," I also think some ideas regarding identity are so rooted in debunked tropes that we *cannot* rescue them. They are no longer the mark of emotional complexity but of reductive conventions.

But outside of the ethical problems raised by getting your details wrong, X, one of the worst problems with treating accuracy as a standard of respectful appropriation is that it treats people as a collection of their material goods, biographical facts, and dialectical tics. It raises journalistic documentation and data to the level of art, rather than complex characterization. What moves me as a reader is something beyond data; it is not accuracy but believability, not exactitude but compassionate approximation. I'm going to suggest that, if you engage in subject appropriation, you will research your characters thoroughly, doing all the intimately engaged critical, historical, literary, and sociological due diligence necessary before committing the details of your character's life to the page. Such research is the basic foundation of both accuracy and truth, but one of the discomfiting things about identity is that it's constructed just outside what components we can document and name. We exist somewhere between our genetic inheritance, our cultural memories, and our physical experiences. We are and are not our maternal languages, our environments and education, our speech patterns and musical taste and clothing choices and sexual desires and religious beliefs. Good writing depends upon showing how a character's psychological and moral sensibilities shift, and her bodily difference can neither finally explain nor rationally locate all these changes. No character is "only" Black or Asian or Latinx. Race informs some level of perception, but it cannot explain every perception, just as it cannot explain every one of a character's actions, beliefs, or desires. All people have behaviors, and there is no set of behaviors intrinsically linked to race.

The final problem with using accuracy as a standard of appropriation is that it demands not just creative fidelity to the details of a community identity, but possibly requires one's own inclusion in that community. Accuracy is assumed to be the province of those who share the identity marker of the written subject, those for whom protecting their community is in their own best psychological and financial interests, since when certain identities are less represented (and represented less positively) than others, the inaccurate appropriation of these voices has long-reaching effects on these communities on and off the page. Simply put, we teach ourselves how to see one another through our figurative representations, and we tend to duplicate these representations over time. You might reasonably argue, then, that to have a character on the page who is embodied differently from the writer risks being not just inherently inaccurate but silencing. For you, the question of whether a character is faithfully or accurately portrayed, then, becomes secondary to the lack of representation *real people* experience in the literary marketplace and in the world.

REPRESENTING VERSUS COMMODIFYING IDENTITIES

Perhaps no recent book exemplifies this problem better than the novel *American Dirt*, by Jeanine Cummins. Published in 2020 to high commercial expectations, *American Dirt* tells the story of a middle-class bookseller, Lydia Quixano Pérez, and her eight-year-old son, Luca, who flee Acapulco after the head of a powerful local cartel, Javier Crespo Fuentes, slaughters Lydia's family in retribution for her journalist husband's articles about him. Cummins received a seven-figure advance for *American Dirt*, and the novel was selected by Oprah's Book Club. Cummins is not Mexican and has, in the past, identified as White, though she is of Irish and Puerto Rican ancestry. After publishing *American Dirt*, Cummins revealed more about her mixed heritage, admitting in the novel's author note that she "wished someone slightly browner" than her would have written the novel, along with hoping that the book might demonstrate that "the people coming to our southern border are not one faceless brown mass but singular individuals."

The Chicana writer Myriam Gurba, in her article, "Pendaja, You Ain't Steinbeck: My Bronca with Fake-Ass Social Justice Literature," took issue with the novel's many inaccuracies, noting also in an interview on NPR's *Latino USA* that no rich and powerful man, like the villain, Javier Fuentes, would woo his girlfriend with conchas, a common Mexican sweet bread, just as no Mexican child would worry about the American bogeyman, but El Cucuy. *American Dirt*, Gurba argued, is not only littered with such cultural inaccuracies but portrays Mexico as primitive, violent, and Third World. All of Gurba's criticisms strike me as simultaneously true and unfair. It's true that Javier brings Lydia conchas, but a few pages later he also arrives with treats from the best chocolatier in Paris. It's true that Mexico is neither primitive nor Third World, but it's also true that violence has displaced many families trying to flee the control of cartels. The landscape Lydia and Luca traverse in *American Dirt* is deliberately populated by homeless migrants, hostels, and derelict train stations so that the two can remain invisible to both the law and their pursuers. The United States, too, is filled with such spaces, and a novel that focused on our own liminal environments would not automatically negate the fact of our nation's modernity.

Reading *American Dirt*, it strikes me that the problem with the novel is not its inaccuracies but its desperately earnest attempts to telegraph Cummins's research. The book opens with a map of Mexico and the southern United States, recalling the maps used in the *Raiders of the Lost Ark* films to help situate American audiences unaware of the location, let alone the existence, of countries like Nepal and Afghanistan. The book then slides in and out of translated Spanish words familiar enough to a general reader that it is unclear why they would need to be included or translated at all, especially by Mexican characters. In the novel's first chapter, for example, Luca, an eight-year-old, notes to himself that "[t]oday is Saturday, April 7, his cousin Yénifer's *quinceañera*, her fifteenth birthday party." Why would Luca need to define for himself the meaning of *quinceañera*? Why also, in the course of two sentences, does Cummins use both the words "*pollo*" and "chicken" for the exact same food?

The book then goes on to include passages like this:

[T]wo dozen law enforcement and medical personnel mov[e] around Abuela's home. . . . Seven receive regular money from the local cartel. The illicit payment is three times more than what they earn from the government . . . Some of the personnel feel morally conflicted about this; others do not. None of them have a choice anyway, so their feelings are largely immaterial. The unsolved-crime rate in Mexico is well north of 90 percent. The costumed existence of *la policia* provides the necessary counterillusion of the cartel's actual impunity.

This passage, though written from an omniscient point of view, is situated in Lydia's perspective just moments after she's seen most of her family slaughtered. A few pages later, Lydia notes that she's witnessed other such crimes, "bodies that are no longer bodies but only parts of bodies, *mutilados* . . . [that are] to set an example, for exaggerated, grotesque illustration."

Do I believe these facts are accurate, both about the mutilation of bodies and the relationship between the police and Mexican cartels? Yes. But I do not believe these facts, and the impassive way these facts are rendered, would be forefront at this moment in Lydia's mind. Who, essentially, are these passages written for?

But even as I write this, X, my criticisms of the novel's clunky factual intrusions feel mean-spirited, insufficient to answering the question of whether the novel is culturally appropriative. As I read *American Dirt*, and the dozens of articles it generated, I must admit there's something bemusing about me, a reader who's not Latinx, arguing what facts and language should compose the authentic internal monologue of a Mexican bookseller fleeing a cartel boss, especially since actual Latina writers like Julia Alvarez, Sandra Cisneros, and Erika Sánchez found the novel believable enough to blurb it. Scrutinizing minor details feels like a particularly loaded game of "Gotcha!" in which every player is destined, at some point, to lose. With enough of the "right" details, shouldn't a writer be able to lure any reader into trusting her, since we each encompass a constellation of behaviors?

If anything, Cummins appears exquisitely attuned to how certain readers might stereotype her characters, and thus paints them in the most irreproachable ways possible. Lydia is highly educated, middle-class and, above all things, a mother. Her passionate protection of Luca is moving and sensitively drawn by Cummins, while it also reinforces the common pro-migrant and -refugee media trope of the refugee as the helpless, docile, and thus easily assimilable subject. Were Luca a sullen teen once recruited by a cartel, not a precocious eight-year-old with a photographic memory and fluent English "learned from YouTube," as Lydia proudly notes; were Lydia herself an unemployed older man, not a bookish and attractive middle-aged woman, a certain reader might find herself more hesitant about wanting this particular parent and child to pass unnoticed through American borders. Cummins's protagonists are women, children, and young teenage girls portrayed as bathetic heroes of a traumatic, but ultimately triumphal, narrative of human survival. To activate our sympathies, they must be marked both by their desperation to reach America and by their suffering, most specifically the suffering done to and not by them, something Luca comes to see as the cement to migrant solidarity itself:

> Luca ... starts to understand that this is the one thing all migrants have in common ... though they all come from different places and different circumstances, some urban, some rural, some middle-class, some poor, some well-educated, some illiterate, Salvadoran, Honduran, Guatemalan, Mexican, Indian, each of them carries some story of suffering on top of that train and into *el norte* beyond.

Suffering both shapes and racially identifies Cummins's characters. After a young, beautiful teen named Soledad is raped by the

Mexican police, an older migrant comforts her by saying she has "the look of a survivor;" Soledad responds by glancing at him, her expression "like [that of] an Aztec warrior." Soledad and her sister Rebeca suffer a barrage of violent encounters that seem to confirm not only their psychological resilience but their commitment to the American project itself. After the sisters cross the border, they grab each other's hands, two girls realizing that, "despite everything they've suffered, at this moment together, they're full of something bigger than hope."

Obviously, the intended audience for *American Dirt* is one that knows little about Mexico, and even less about the migrant crisis; one, perhaps, that views the United States in ways similar to Soledad and Rebeca. To be fair, Cummins never portrays Americans here as White saviors—or even sympathetic characters—but she also doesn't address any of the natural hesitations a character like Lydia should feel about fleeing to a nation that's defined by its anti-migrant rhetoric. Instead, the United States is simply an endpoint to be reached, a strangely depoliticized space of physical and psychic respite that serves as a haven to those strong enough to reach it. In that, *American Dirt* appeals to readers who want to thrill to the plight of imperiled characters while never having to question their own political connection to the migrants imagined on the page.

American Dirt was described by early reviewers as an update of John Steinbeck's *Grapes of Wrath*, though a better comparison might be *Uncle Tom's Cabin*, as other critics have suggested, since the novel functions as a melodrama meant to convert indifferent readers to racially progressive views. Reading *American Dirt* in 2020, I was reminded of James Baldwin's 1966 essay, "Everybody's Protest Novel," which excoriates *Uncle Tom's Cabin* for its sentimentality: a mark, Baldwin wrote, of the novel's essential "dishonesty, [its] inability to feel." This dishonesty is due to the fact that the novel is "not intended to do anything more than prove slavery was wrong; was, in fact, perfectly horrible." As such, the novel leaves untouched the Christian theology that suffuses its fictional world, a theology that fosters violent racist hierarchies even as Stowe herself critiques Christian-led slavery. *Uncle Tom's Cabin* protests slavery but does nothing to dismantle the spiritual and aesthetic ideals that reify racist paradigms.

Baldwin argued that protest novels like *Uncle Tom's Cabin*, and now *American Dirt*, are "meant to be comforting" to readers because they rarely confront conservative values, preferring instead to function as "mirrors of our confusion, dishonesty, panic," the novels themselves "trapped and immobilized in the sunlit prison of the American Dream." It is that faint imprint of the American Dream amberized at the heart of Cummins's novel that galls and excites, its suggestion that Cummins's beautiful, traumatized migrants might be free inside our borders, while never presenting a whiff of critique for a system that demonizes and depends upon migrant labor.

For these very reasons, interestingly, many critics accused *American Dirt* of being "trauma porn" because the novel, in order to engage readers of all political stripes, avoids more complex characterization in favor of sensational plot. The novel does not rely on any figuration of the literal events Cummins depicts; instead, *American Dirt* is a trophic cascade of violence set off by a massacre at a family barbecue. The novel is a thriller, and as with many thrillers it sticks to conventions of genre. Minimal detail is spent on psychological development, while maximum detail is expended on violence that excites the reader while proving Cummins has done her research. And the details are sensational. Women are raped, people are shot, migrants die or are crushed while falling from La Bestia, and all these things happen in a relentless succession of details that feel at once both highly believable and finally meaningless. Violent events exist only to activate our sympathies, not our critical reimagining of the characters, nor what underpins the migrant crisis itself.

I wrote earlier that works of cultural appropriation traffic, consciously or not, in racist metaphors. But reading *American Dirt*, I discovered there are equally problems with appropriative texts that traffic in no metaphors at all. Metaphor is crucial to structuring narrative, X, because a situation must exist in the text that's larger than the one immediately presented us as readers for us to differentiate story from plot. In *American Dirt*, the border, for Cummins, is literally the border; there is little sense that border crossing could symbolically reflect any of the characters' internal states, even as Lydia herself changes from a middle-class, happily married woman to a traumatized and near-penniless widow. Lydia, Luca, Rebeca, and Soledad may not be, as Cummins insists, members of "a faceless brown mass," but because Cummins centers her novel solely on the *activity* of these characters' border crossing rather than the *metaphor* of their crossing, she makes them feel like statistics.

APPROPRIATION AS REPRESENTATIVE THINKING

Compare Cummins's characterization of Lydia with the novelist Lisa Halliday's depiction of an Iraqi American man named Amar Ala Jaafari in her novel *Asymmetry* and you'll see the profound difference between metaphoric story and plot. Like Cummins, Halliday also writes about border crossing, since Amar, the protagonist of the novel section titled "Madness," is being detained in Heathrow while trying to visit a British friend. But borders in "Madness" take on increasingly resonant meanings as the novel unfolds. Amar, for example, is literally a man born between nations, since his mother gave birth to him on an airplane. Amar also lacks a coherent and cohesive memory; his most vivid recollections are in fact supplied to him by his brother, who's told Amar what he should remember, so that Amar's very sense of self feels increasingly porous. In that, Amar is a liminal figure who belongs nowhere, has no clearly determined identity, and possesses an education and job that let him travel widely. Amar's cosmopolitanism allows him to travel along the margins of many different societies while also making him the unwitting victim of America's war on terrorism. He's detained by the British because of his dual citizenship, an act of bureaucratic racial profiling that reveals how powerless Amar's fluid identity finally makes him.

Like Cummins, Halliday does not share her character's ethnic or racial background, and like Cummins, Halliday includes specific details to make her depiction feel both accurate and authentic. Amar references religious traditions and holidays, makes note of his incomplete knowledge of Iraqi history, and ponders his experience of being othered in both America and Iraq. These details, however, are included not as plot points but as something natural to Amar's personal story; Amar does not have to explain their meaning because Amar narrates his story in first person. Amar thus addresses both us *and* himself, and because of that, "Madness" does not forecast that it is written for a non-Muslim audience.

Most important, however, Halliday includes the story of Amar because *Asymmetry* is an examination of unbalanced authority. The first section of the novel, "Folly," focuses on a young book editor, Alice, who's quietly learning to become a writer. Alice dates a far more famous and established male novelist named Ezra Blazer, who alternates between condescending to Alice and mentoring her creatively. "Madness," in contrast, is about Amar recognizing how the uneven relationship between America and Iraq have both global and personal effects. If it is "folly" for a young woman to try to change the desires of a more powerful man, it is certainly "madness" for an Iraqi-American to imagine he can explain his identity to the British border control in a post-9/11 world. Throughout her novel, Halliday examines the ways that unequal forms of power—whether sexual, racial, political, artistic, interpersonal, or global—frame the experiences of individuals in ways they cannot fully express or control.

But Halliday does something else as well. If the first part of *Asymmetry* is a roman à clef—Halliday herself worked in publishing and once dated Philip Roth—she drops clues throughout the novel that suggest Alice is in fact the author of "Madness." In that, Halliday telegraphs to the reader that we are *never* meant to read Amar's story as his own, but as another metatextual attempt at both Alice's story and Halliday's biography. In fact, it is the novel's Philip Roth character, Ezra Blazer, who suggests at the end of *Asymmetry* that "Madness," like all novels, was written to "reduce the blind spots" in its author's own life, and that the character Amar "would seem to have nothing to do with [his] author, but in fact is a kind of veiled portrait of someone determined to transcend her provenance, her privilege, her naiveté."

Blazer suggests that it is through fiction that we get closer not to other people, but to the private truths of our own lives. Just as Amar uses the memories of his brother to construct his own life story, Halliday slyly uses the imagined life of Amar to better express the lives of Alice and herself. *Asymmetry,* then, is not attempting to individuate one Iraqi American from a "faceless brown mass"; it has no sentimental project, thus it does not try to engage the sympathies of readers unfamiliar to Muslim Americans. Rather Halliday uses Amar, Alice, and Blazer himself to explore the ways that writing, too, is deeply tied to power and representation. *Asymmetry* is not an argument for empathy in fiction exactly; rather, it is an example of Hannah Arendt's ideas of "representative thinking" at work. In "Madness," we are to see Alice's, and thus Halliday's, own consciousness shaped and refracted by the experiences Amar would have had to live in "real" life.

Both *American Dirt* and *Asymmetry* are obviously works of subject appropriation. But only *American Dirt*'s appropriations feel questionable to me, not because the writing itself devolves into racist caricatures, but because its melodramatic structure and insistence on documentary realism require that I take Lydia's story more seriously than Amar's. *American Dirt* was sold, published, and promoted on the idea that our empathetic identification with Lydia would make American readers care about the plight of actual migrants. *Asymmetry* does not ask us to identify with anyone, but to consider how we construct ourselves through narrative. Halliday makes no claim to speak for or about Iraqi Americans, as Amar's struggle to articulate his life under interrogation is due to the "madness" of post-9/11 politics, not because Amar himself is inarticulate. In contrast, Cummins wrote in her author's note that she wanted to "be a bridge," another voice in the chorus of those "telling this story." Cummins is not claiming to speak for others, exactly, but she certainly wants to speak alongside them.

And this desire to speak alongside other Latinx authors requires me then to consider whether Cummins's presence diminishes their voices. In this case, regardless of how respectful or accurately researched Cummins's characters may be, her portrayal of these characters, and her own White identity, become commodities within our publication system. This is something the writer Sandra Cisneros, who blurbed *American Dirt* positively, even argued was a strength about the novel, saying it was the book's genre along with Cummins's White surname that would bring readers uninterested in serious literature about the border to this topic. People who might be "turned off" from books written by Latinx authors whose subject matters they might deem too ethnic or political might, Cisneros speculated on *Latino USA*, be persuaded by *American Dirt* to reconsider how America treats migrants. In that, Cisneros sees *American Dirt* as a "Trojan Horse" that can change the minds of readers Cisneros herself never hoped to reach.

I find Cisneros's argument both canny and cynical, and it illuminates for me exactly why Latinx authors are hurt by the marketplace success of *American Dirt*. On Facebook and Twitter, I read countless threads from Latinx writer friends who've struggled to publish books, only to be told by agents and editors that their stories about the border are too dark, too difficult, or not commercial enough. Their personal experiences are borne out by data and also shared by other underrepresented groups. The 2020 viral hashtag #Publishing-PaidMe recently unveiled the stark difference in publication advances between Black and non-Black authors. Likewise, researchers at the Stanford University Literary Lab discovered that not only does 86 percent of the publishing industry identify as White, but both book acquisition rates and book advances are lower for writers of color because publishers don't consider their target audience significant enough to generate popular interest. This assessment is based on the fact that the majority of "comps" or "comparative" titles editors use to determine a publication's market value are White-authored.

Thus what people are angry about, X, is that a marketplace determines whose stories sound "authentic" enough to deserve money and a readership. They're angry that having a Latinx name apparently means having only one subject matter and political opinion, and that editors don't seem eager to prove this assumption false. For them, Cummins's Whiteness was exactly what made this novel so attractive to its publishing house, because it meant a larger and ethnically wider audience, and it pandered to a readership that didn't want to be politically or aesthetically challenged.

In that sense, the publishing world's embrace of *American Dirt* absolutely occurs at the expense of Latinx authors, since Cummins is granted the appearance of more creative and political freedom. By making *American Dirt* an Oprah's Book Club selection, or pushing it to get large trade reviews, or placing it prominently in bookstores and airports, the publishing world reinforces the belief that people don't need or want to hear what Latinx authors, and Latinx people, have to say. If you and I can agree that the human imagination is never free of human bodies, X, we need also to recognize that literary texts can never be sheared of their historical context, aesthetic affiliations, and political readings. When critics accuse *American Dirt* of being culturally appropriative, it's because they understand how literature has been historically used to enforce particular patterns of power. In that, it is not the depiction of race on the page, but the ways colonial history continues to shape publication policy that offends people. We might call the publication and promotion of *American Dirt* then a kind of marketplace colonialism.

So is this all Cummins's fault? No. She is just a random if extraordinarily well-remunerated recipient of White privilege in the publishing industry. And while I myself have no great love for this novel, I must admit I feel queasy critiquing it, since I suspect that

Cummins has become the stand-in for arguments her novel could never solve, even as it raises them. When we write books that appropriate the experiences and identities of other people, X, we enter into a system in which we all participate but over which we individually have very little control. The publication of Cummins's book, even as its author and editors rebuke the rhetoric that shapes U.S. border policy, participates in the racial hierarchies that have also informed that policy, which is why the backlash against *American Dirt* feels both historically justified and personally unfair. But when faced with the enormity of our institutions whose actions implicate us, X, I think it's easy to direct our fury at the representatives of these institutions rather than demand the institutions change themselves. It's certainly easier to criticize *American Dirt* than to expect the United States will reinvent its immigration policy, or that publishers will dismantle our current publication system, or that politicians will free migrant children incarcerated at the border.

Thus part of the queasiness I experience when reading *American Dirt* has to do with feeling manipulated on all sides. If I like the novel, does that mean I'm an easy mark for its sentimentality, or that perhaps I harbor racist fantasies about Mexico? If I dislike the book, what does my anger do but bring me into community with other like-minded critics on the Internet? If I can't do much practically for children separated from their parents at the border, or ensure my Latinx friends get bigger advances, I can at least signal my political sympathies by vilifying the book on Twitter. My anger at the novel would be, I see, a little like the lesson offered by the narrator in Carlson-Wee's poem: I could make the act of my reading perform the values I want other people to see in me.

MARKETPLACE COLONIALISM AND APPROPRIATION

The outrage surrounding *American Dirt* returns us to the fact that cultural appropriation is not strictly a problem of creative fidelity but also of remuneration. Because by taking on the stories of another group and using these stories as the basis for work you sell as your own, X, you profit from the labor of another person or group. By making a name off this work you've profited from, you further your own reputation at the cost of shrinking that of the original artists. And finally, by reproducing these stories in your own work, you've helped frame for future audiences the "authentic" narratives that should define the group you've appropriated.

Which is why you and I must remember there are two essential debates lodged within the question of appropriation: one is whether it can be done, and one is whether it *should* be done. But while these debates are connected, I think they are also, at some fundamental point, different. Whether you or I can write in another's voice attentively depends upon how you and I imagine the experience of difference to be "authentic"; how much you and I believe the imagination can be expanded through desire; and how much our critical studies of literature, race, and culture might contribute positively to these representations. If, however, you don't believe anyone should write in another's voice out of respect for the problems of racial inequality and colonialism that are preserved in our publishing system, or until we have achieved social equality in civic life, then art, skill, and research don't matter. These are distant concerns to the desire to let people control their own narratives.

Of course, representation in art and in life are themselves

linked. More representations by people of color of themselves allow for more diverse artists to thrive. Representation on the page, in the editorial room, and outside on the street all matter, because they go hand-in-hand.

Perhaps, X, based on the enduring problems of social inequality, you are skeptical that any artist writing outside her identity position could avoid racist fantasies. Or perhaps you know that from our nation's earliest origins, literacy was policed; certain areas of the country even made teaching slaves to read and write a finable offense. Thus you understand that a historic, triangulated relationship exists in our nation between literary production, race, and economic alienation. In a culture that consistently rewards the White imagination and its artistic productions at the expense of artists of color, any ethical choice you might make is fundamentally constrained. With these realities in mind, you might argue that the only option with regard to appropriation is to opt out.

So here's the question, X: do you opt out?

Obviously, only you can answer this question, but I'd like to trouble the assumption that opting out is the only anti-racist position you can take. Frankly, I don't believe that an artist writing outside her subject position can only write into racist stereotypes. Racist stereotypes are pervasive, perhaps almost automatic to our thinking, but that doesn't mean we can't train ourselves to recognize and combat them. The fact that we do not popularly duplicate in our literature now the same language about people of color that appeared two hundred years ago is a testament to that. As I wrote before, I have to believe we can educate ourselves to reject racial hierarchies and meanings. If I can change my mind about William Meredith's poem, others can as well.

I also think this argument risks replicating the far right's reasoning around identity, which is to suggest that certain groups are too essentially different from the majority to be understood. If the far right argues that the other is inhuman, the far left now seems to think the other is unimaginable. Neither is a satisfying proposition, nor is it one that takes into consideration our complexly intertwined histories. Even as Edward Said recognized the profound ways people from the West dehumanized people from the East, for example, he also argued that we must "acknowledge the massively knotted . . . histories of special but nevertheless overlapping and interconnected experiences—of women, of Westerners, of Blacks, of national states and cultures—there is no particular intellectual reason for granting each and all of them an ideal and essentially separate status."

As to the argument that you should not write outside your subject position because we do not have equality in the world or in the publishing system, I'm more persuaded. In some sense, this argument is total and undebatable. The racial bias we experience in our lives affects the literary world. Writers of color remain less reviewed, less institutionally supported, less likely to work in publishing. We are diversifying our literature, but we have not worked hard enough as a community to ensure that people are equally enfranchised in the classroom, in the publishing houses, and on the fancy tables at the bookstores. Diversity is solved by having more bodies in the room and on the page. Equality is solved when people with historically less power take an equal share of the decision-making with those who've historically had more.

And yet, while this argument may be irrefutable, I believe it also relies on an assumption that hasn't entirely panned out either, which is that *only* writing by people of color can address and defeat our culture's essentialist tropes about race, and that White writers can't effectively be anti-racist in their writing. If you think that, read Jess Row or Eula Biss or Martha Collins or Robin DiAngelo. If you resist appropriation out of respect for social equality and history, that's a profoundly ethical choice, X, but it will have to be an individual one, since it can't be institutionally enforced in a country that values and protects freedom of speech. And, of course, if you wait for social equality to sanction your appropriation, you'll be waiting a *very* long time. And what will that equality look like, exactly? What are its exact terms and conditions? How many working writers and editors of color in the publishing industry will satisfy you? How many scholars and curators and tastemakers and reviewers? What number and world will persuade you, when we must always dream of better and of more?

As you can see, the pervasive and often invisible history of colonialism that persists in our culture means that the discussion around appropriation inevitably devolves into a debate about cultural enfranchisement. These discussions, while based on different arguments, share a common concern about representative control. Perhaps I might argue that seeing the world through the eyes of a person unlike myself is a way to expand such control, in which case, respectful forms of appropriation might combat racism by showing how people are linked and not just divided by arbitrary social codes. But as long as we have reproduced and continue to reproduce these social meanings around race off the page, I think it's irresponsible to declare that literary appropriation can act as a social panacea. It might help change, but it will not entirely cure a system of thought that affects our political, social, and artistic institutions.

This is why, X, an appropriative work that succeeds aesthetically might also be treated by readers as a larger ethical failure, and why appropriative works can never be excused or justified on the basis of accuracy. If you are looking for comfort or vindication for your writing, you will never have it. You will have to choose for yourself, understanding that even sensitive literary portrayals may perpetuate racist systems.

I wrote before that to turn the discussion of literary appropriation into a yes/no debate would stultify nuance, forcing us into defending unrealistic or calcified positions. It would also suggest, however, that there is only one set of values we should hold about literature, which is how it depicts and resists race-based systems of power. But that's not all we come to literature for, and that's certainly not the only critical rubric through which we read poems and stories. If anything, the question of appropriation should remind us that, if literature can never be separated from the society in which it is produced, our practice of reading, then, should not be treated as the simple revelation of archetypal "human" values, fears, and ambitions but a critical response to see how we've socially constructed ideas of humanness itself.

But if literature is subject to history and politics, I think we can see how the reverse is also true, as it is through imaginative writing that readers start renegotiating the terms in which institutions depict them. We may look askance now, for example, at the aesthetic project of *Uncle Tom's Cabin*, but that novel had a powerful and positive effect on American attitudes toward Black Americans, swelling support for the abolitionist movement and helping lay the foundation for the Civil War. That said, as the critic Jess Row noted in his *Los Angeles Times* essay on *American Dirt*, the 1978 dystopian novel *The Turner Diaries*, by William Luther Pierce, had a massive social impact as well, with its depiction of a race war that leads to the extermination of White people serving as the inspiration for the

1995 Oklahoma City bombings, the 1999 London nail bombings, and even the 1984 murder of the liberal radio host Alan Berg. Like *Uncle Tom's Cabin*, *The Turner Diaries* had a galvanizing effect on American readers—only these ones were in the White nationalist movement.

My point, X, is that sentimental fiction can move us in any direction that the author wants. Literature is not an automatically innocent or socially progressive pursuit because it is creative, and what's at stake when we write is not only self-expression or imaginative freedom, which is what Lionel Shriver suggests in her speeches. Writing is a profoundly unsettling tool, which we overlook when we categorize appropriation as an elaborate act of empathy or when we treat literary characters as mere expressions of didactic values. As Baldwin wrote in "Everybody's Protest Novel," a true character

> is not, after all, merely a member of a Society or a Group or a deplorable conundrum to be explained by Science. He is—and how old-fashioned the words sound!—something more than that, something resolutely indefinable, unpredictable . . . It is this power of [character] revelation which is the business of the novelist, this journey toward a more vast reality which must take precedence over all other claims.

In that, perhaps we might find in the most compelling appropriations a trace of that "indefinable, unpredictable" essence of self, especially when these works demonstrate how people are both the subjects and authors of the histories that constrain them. Compassionate approximations, if they want to avoid becoming cultural appropriations, cannot first be sentimental projects. As writers, we are both passive and active agents of the state, colonizers and the colonized, outsiders and insiders to the systems and identities we critique. Does writing in the voice of another help or worsen these conditions? Does it mute other writers we wish to speak alongside of, or does it bring more voices into the conversation?

The answer is both, X, at the very same time.

LETTER FOUR

Identity as Encounter

Dear X:

So, when it comes to compassionate approximations of racial identity in literature, what is truth? Or, more to the point, what feels like a truthful depiction of race?

Returning to *The Confessions of Nat Turner* for a moment, one of the things I *do* admire about the novel is how flexible, at times, Turner's identity becomes. In Styron's hands, Turner is both friend and slave, man and not-man, religious devotee and political revolutionary. Throughout his many interactions with both White and Black people, Nat Turner comes to a painful and often nuanced understanding of his position as a Black man in the South, and the continuing misery of Styron's novel lies in the ways Turner is forced to see himself as others see him. In one early passage, Turner describes this awareness of his racial meaning as being a certain inward sense—an essence of being which is almost impossible to put into words—that every Negro possesses when, dating from the age of twelve or ten or even earlier, he becomes aware that he is only merchandise, goods, in the eyes of all white people devoid of character or moral sense or soul. This feeling Hark called "black-assed," and it comes as close to summing up the numbness and dread which dwells in every Negro's heart as any word I have ever known.

Turner understands that his racial meaning is relational; his identity consistently enforces certain choices upon him, though not always the same ones. Turner's agency is thus continually in flux, and in this way Styron's novel suggests that race is less a question of bodily difference than psychic possibility: we are raced when we become aware of how our world encourages or discourages certain options for us.

When I read this passage in Styron's novel, X, I began to wonder what would change in our discussion of appropriation if we didn't think about race as a specific physical or even psychological identity but an encounter, one that suddenly provided us with an alternate view of ourselves. This is something W.E.B. Du Bois asked in his 1903 book *The Souls of Black Folk*, in which he describes the predicament he terms "double consciousness" faced by African Americans who must see themselves as "American, [and] Negro; two souls, two thoughts, two unreconciled strivings; two warring ideals in one body." Racism, Du Bois argues, robs African Americans of the ability to see themselves without first seeing how they are seen by White people: in that way, African Americans can see themselves only "through the revelation of the other world." Double consciousness is not a mark of innate Black psychic disorientation but a result of years of White racial prejudice and violence that has been both observed and suffered by African Americans, who come to realize the depth of their exclusion from American nationhood and may also internalize these stereotypes. In certain respects, double consciousness may actually clarify, rather than confuse African American identity, as African Americans become excruciatingly aware of the ways they come to mean and suggest different identities depending on the context in which they are observed.

While Du Bois's description of double consciousness was specifically written to apply to Black identity, I would argue that double consciousness is experienced by any person who does not share the racial, cultural, physical, or sexual identity of her nation's majority, whose sense of self risks being split into warring sides based on negative perceptions of her outward appearance or social meaning. Our sense of being "othered" is essentially relational, as these other selves come into view when witnessed by particular audiences.

RACE AS RELATIONAL METAPHOR

Here's an example of how race becomes relational. It's the opening passage from "The Hull Case," a short story by the Chinese-Welsh writer Peter Ho Davies.

> Helen is telling the colonel about the ship now, and Henry, sitting stiffly on the sectional sofa beside his wife, can't look up. He stares at the colonel's cap, the gold braid on the rim, where it rests on the coffee table next to the latest *Saturday Evening Post* and the plate of tunafish sandwiches Helen has laid out.

"What color were the lights, Mrs. Hull?" the colonel wants to know, and Helen says, "Blue."

The colonel makes a check mark.

"Baby blue," Helen adds. She looks at Henry, and he nods quickly. He thought the lights were a cop at first.

"The Hull Case" tells the story of a mixed-race couple living in New Hampshire in the early 1960s who become the subjects of one of the earliest reported UFO abductions in North America. "The Hull Case" is told from the point of view of Henry Hull, who is African American.

Of course, we aren't told that Henry is Black until the end of the first section of the story. Davies drops this information in two terse paragraphs that suggest Henry's quiet tension about his marriage, his acute sense of the threat Helen's racial difference makes to his life. Here is what Davies writes:

> Henry thought the lights were a cop at first. They'd already been stopped once on the drive back from Niagara. He could have sworn he'd been doing less than sixty. The cop had shone his flashlight in Henry's face—black—and then Helen's—white.
>
> "Any trouble here, ma'am?"
>
> "Not at all, officer," she told him, while Henry gripped the wheel with both hands.

Notice that Davies repeats Henry's thinking that the UFO lights were a cop's. Notice, too, that Henry sits "stiffly," that he takes in the colonel's military regalia, that Helen does all the talking and has—with her platter of tuna-fish sandwiches—obviously thought of this meeting as a friendly visit. Henry and Helen's differences in temperament and in their relationship to authority are entirely opposite. Henry was in the military (which explains his close attention to the colonel's braid), but he's also experienced a world Helen hasn't, one that's characterized by surveillance and segregation. But this meeting with the colonel is in Helen's world, on Helen's terms. Henry doesn't resent his wife, but he also can't share Helen's optimism. Even though she's a woman, Helen has always been treated with some level of deference, and her stubbornness has gotten her what she's wanted—even her marriage to Henry, which her parents at first weakly protested but, Helen insists, "They kn[ew] better than to try to stop me when I want something."

That line is a powerful way to encapsulate the many complications hidden within Helen's privilege. Helen is, at once, to be admired for her willfulness that lets her love whomever and as she will, but she's also to be criticized for her equally willful myopia. As the story unfolds, Helen can't seem to believe the colonel wouldn't believe her: if she saw a UFO, why should he doubt it? Henry, on the other hand, is used to possessing knowledge no one in power believes. When he tries to warn Helen that reporting their UFO abduction will get them in trouble, or make them a laughingstock, Helen scolds him for "having no gumption." In reality, Henry's accustomed to not being heard, and the bitter pill of the story is that Helen—whom he loves—also doesn't hear him.

Over and over in Davies's story, we see how Helen's decisions have painful consequences for Henry. Helen's White parents grudgingly accept their marriage, Henry's Black family refuse to attend the wedding. Helen sees their UFO abduction as an opportunity to share an important scientific discovery; Henry experiences their abduction, and Helen's reporting of it, as another moment of humiliation.

Peter Ho Davies is a Chinese-Welsh, Anglo-American writer. He's not African American, and he never lived in America during the 1960s. So why does the story—and Henry—convince me as being truthful? First, "The Hull Case," from its start, telegraphs its obsession with color and difference: Helen and the colonel go back and forth about the exact color of the lights, Henry is fixated on the colonel's gold braid. Color represents truth, authority, accuracy, and perception to these characters, and this metaphor extends not just through the descriptions in the story of other objects and events, it extends to the racial perceptions and experiences of the two main characters. Color even suggests the mixed-race child Helen longs to have and Henry fears will actually arrive: "baby blue," Helen calls the UFO lights, while Henry returns to thinking about the cops. It's not just that Henry's negative expectations of White authority are historically believable, they subtly structure the interactions Henry has with the other White characters. Davies shows us how race informs the many gestures each character makes, and though Helen and the colonel may be more obtuse than Henry about the privilege they possess, they, too, are shaped by race and awareness of racial difference. Even the aliens' skin is racialized by the colonel, who, when informed by Helen that the aliens were "gray," repeats the word while flicking his eyes back and forth between Helen and Henry.

And yet this awareness of racial meaning and difference, while pervasive in the story, does not reduce these characters to archetypes. Henry possesses a complex set of feelings for Helen, whose "innocence," as he calls it, both infuriates him and inspires his protection. He does not want to lose his wife, whether to divorce, or to complications from childbirth, or to the social forces working to undermine them. Henry wants Helen to have a child, since it will please Helen, even as he himself is filled with dread at the prospect of raising a mixed-race child in America. Henry is suspicious and loving and protective and pessimistic and optimistic and lonely in his marriage, all at once. Race inspires and explains many of these emotions, but it does not explain all of them.

This is what I mean by race as relational, and what Du Bois meant by double consciousness. Henry's choices throughout the story are continually shaped by how people—including Henry himself—see race and gender. Henry doesn't perform or conform to any one stereotypical idea of Blackness, even as he is aware that stereotypes about his identity exist. Instead, Henry's actions work to quietly undermine the White male characters' assumptions about him while also placating and protecting his naïve wife. Henry is resilient, skeptical, loving, and resistant. He's a person, not a caricature.

The complexity and contradictions of consciousness Henry demonstrates in "The Hull Case" is entirely different from that of Nick Adams in Ernest Hemingway's famous short story "Indian Camp." In "Indian Camp," Nick, his father, and his uncle George are being rowed by some young Native American men to the "Indian camp" of the title, where a young Native woman is having trouble giving birth. Nick's father, a doctor, helps the woman deliver by giving her a C-section, "[w]ith a jack knife," as he brags to his brother, George, after "sew[ing] it up with nine-foot, tapered gut leaders." The "it" refers to the C-section, though you might be forgiven for thinking the pronoun refers to the Native woman, as Nick's father never addresses her, she's given no name, and is throughout the story treated as an object whose feelings have little effect on Nick's father. At one point, the young woman screams in pain, and Nick asks his father whether he can give her an anesthetic. "No," his father replies. "I haven't any aesthetic . . . But her screams are not important. I don't hear them because they are not important."

Hemingway's style is, of course, famously spare, so it shouldn't surprise you that his Native characters receive little to no psychological development. Nick Adams, his father, and Uncle George are lightly sketched, too, though I understand through Hemingway's repeated description of Nick "refusing to look" at the woman's operation and his father's rough delivery of the child that Nick is disgusted by the scene, and likely by what the birth comes to represent: female reproduction, Indian racial "otherness," his father's callous medical work. In "Indian Camp," White people literally block off their senses so that the distress of the Native woman cannot be heard or perceived. Nick's father thinks her screams are "not important," while Nick refuses to look at his father stitching her up, even turning away from the child his father "puts in the basin," his curiosity "gone for a long time." Nick's numbness is in part echoed by the woman herself, who, after her surgery, lies back, "quiet now and [with] her eyes . . . closed. She did not know what had become of the baby or anything."

One emotion that does register to all the characters, however, is contempt. When the woman bites Nick's uncle George as he holds her forcibly down for the surgery, he snaps, calling her a "Damn squaw bitch!" at which point one of the young male Native Americans laughs, delighted she has wounded this White stranger.

Disdain is the presiding emotion of Hemingway's story, as David Treuer notes in his talk on cultural appropriation at the 2018 Bread Loaf Writers' Conference, and it's largely the disdain Hemingway's White characters feel for Native suffering. For the real climax of the story is not the Native woman's C-section but the suicide of her husband, who slits his throat ear to ear with a razor blade, miraculously without making a sound. Treuer argues this is a continuation of the story's objectification of Native people; that the casual, absolutely incidental addition of the husband's death reifies his essential inhumanness to Hemingway's White observers, a suggestion supported by the fact that, when Nick asks his father why the man committed suicide, his father replies, "I don't know. He couldn't stand things, I guess."

What do you think these "things" are that the man couldn't stand, X? Witnessing his wife's pain? The fact that White strangers are holding his wife down as they cut her? The fact he himself suffers from an ax wound left untreated in his foot? Life itself? Life as an American Indian man? Life as a man in general? Having read the story many times, I can't say. Hemingway's clipped style suggests that two or more of these options are possible, and certainly Nick's father makes a clear distinction between male and female suicide, telling Nick that women "hardly ever" kill themselves, as opposed to men, who do it more often. And though I agree with Treuer that the story is soaked with indifference for its Native characters, none of whom speaks a single word in this story, I can also see that "Indian Camp" struggles to suggest there's something more than the normal medical callousness common to doctors in Nick's father. George and Nick's father are, at heart, racists. Nick, a child in the story, is being shaped by their racist, callous, and androcentric vision of life. Nick is guilty of objectifying the Native woman too, of course, of looking away. But the story suggests that Nick might also be growing aware of his father's limitations, and that part of what he doesn't want to see in this Indian camp is what kind of man his father really is.

The story is both awful and compelling. What makes it culturally appropriative is not just the White characters' essential disdain for the Native Americans, nor the fact that the Native characters lack any kind of individuality, humanity, or agency, it's the fact that Hemingway also reduces them to suffering and suicide. In this story, pain is the metonym for being American Indian, as all the Native characters are either wounded, suffering, or taking delight in another's wounding. They have no active relationship with anyone. Instead, they are defined by their death, a trope that would have been familiar to American readers in the 1920s when "Indian Camp" was first published, having seen this theme repeated in many American literary and artistic works. Here is a 1911 poem by the American poet Ella Rhoads Higginson:

THE VANISHING RACE

Into the shadow, whose illumined crest
    Speaks of the world behind them where the sun
    Still shines for us whose day is not yet done,
Those last dark ones go drifting. East or West,
Or North or South—it matters not; their quest
    Is toward the shadow whence it was begun;
    Hope in it, Ah, my brothers; there is none;
And yet—they only seek a place to rest.

So mutely, uncomplainingly, they go!
    How shall it be with us when they are gone,
    When they are but a mem'ry and a name?

May not those mournful eyes to phantoms grow—
        When, wronged and lonely, they have drifted on
        Into the voiceless shadow whence they came?

It's a terrible poem that popularly expressed a sentiment common to American readers, cultural anthropologists, and photographers in the early twentieth century, which is that American Indians were a race of people who, from the beginning of American history, were doomed to extinction. Higginson's title comes from the photographer Edward Sheriff Curtis's 1904 photograph *The Vanishing Race*, which depicts a group of Navajo riding—literally—into the sunset, their darkened backs turned to the viewer. Such "noble savages," Curtis's elegiac photo suggests, simply couldn't survive encroaching modern American life. The Vanishing Race was a common literary and visual trope in American literature because it excused and encouraged American expansion westward; it allowed for Native people to be rounded up and put in reservations; and it forgave American legislators their acts of duplicity, theft, and murder. It celebrated the beauty of Native Americans by elegizing them; it treated them as objects to be mourned, idealized, admired, and forgotten.

Finally, and perhaps most important, the Vanishing Race trope allowed for and encouraged the work of White artists to document the pain, suffering, death, and disappearance of Native peoples: it offered White artists a moral lens through which to view their own aesthetic projects. In that sense, X, you might look at the subtle interrogation "Indian Camp" makes of its own racism (if you in fact believe it *is* interrogating its own racism) as yet another act of self-congratulation. Indians may be voiceless savages marked for obsolescence, Hemingway suggests, but at least I'm sensitive enough—and man enough—to endure that knowledge.

Hemingway's story is a perfect example of race as negative metaphor. In Hemingway's story, American Indians aren't people, they're symbols of a familiar social allegory about the preordained erasure of Native people. Hemingway's minimalist prose only accentuates the absence of interiority the Native characters possess. Because they aren't given room to speak, they provide me with no historical or ideological context that might change how I perceive them as people: the story's style drains and empties them. Like the White characters, the Native characters are defined by action, but unlike the White characters they are defined by actions that happen *to* them. Even the man's suicide takes place in the shadows, reminding me that the literal definition of "obscene" is "offstage," and that Nick's refusal to look at the Native woman's surgery, her birth, and pain suggests that he finds all these things obscene. In "Indian Camp," Native suffering, life, agency, and interiority become a kind of obscene metaphor I do not have to witness. It stands in stark contrast to Davies's story, in which color becomes a metaphor for how people see the world; race and color function not as static symbols but as aspects of character that are in flux, because one's character is formed in relation to others. Hemingway's story is appropriative not because it dares to include Native characters, but because Hemingway doesn't let these Native characters dare to become human.

Returning to Du Bois's argument about double consciousness here, what if, when writing about other people, I locate race as the marker that informs my character's actions in the text but is not itself reinforced by that character's activity and labor in the world?

In other words, how is race not a figurative symbol for a social value but a shifting point of reference? I recognize that I'm still using race as a metaphor, this time for the experience of being split into multiple consciousnesses. But this way of reading race insists upon its active properties. Racist metaphors negate agency; they require a singular and dehumanizing vision of the raced person, rendering that person an object. Race as a relational metaphor, however, asks that we consider the ways that racial meaning changes as the individual in her moment-to-moment context changes.

There's a novel I think that achieves this perfectly, titled *China Mountain Zhang*, a little-known work of speculative fiction published in 1992 by Maureen F. McHugh. *China Mountain Zhang* is a strange novel-in-stories that I teach in my advanced Asian American literature classes, much to the surprise of my students, because it's not by an Asian American author. *China Mountain Zhang* episodically follows a group of people "caught in the cracks," as McHugh writes, denizens of a world in which China has now become the dominant global force. China's success means that it has now colonized Europe and the United States, forcing the United States to undergo its own Communist revolution after its economic collapse, all while luring the Chinese diaspora back to China's shores. In McHugh's world, people across the globe now flock to Beijing and Shanghai for jobs, education, and a more secure lifestyle; many even undergo plastic surgery to make their physical features look more Asian. The protagonist, a mixed-race man named China Mountain Zhang, undergoes such a surgery himself to hide his mother's "less desirable" Puerto Rican ancestry, but even though he looks fully Chinese and can blend in visually, he can never forget the fact that he's gay—still a social and legal taboo in China, where he briefly emigrates.

Maureen F. McHugh is a white American woman from Ohio. From interviews I've read, I've learned she spent a year teaching in China, but she's certainly not a China expert, nor is she mixed race, male or, apparently, gay. And yet her novel absorbs me because it never tries to pinpoint what it means to be gay or Chinese or mixed race or even male; instead, it is a compelling look at how all identities get shaped by media, technology, globalism, and money.

From an American perspective, perhaps you and I might read a future ruled by Communist China as dystopian, but what McHugh shows me is that this fictional world looks strangely familiar. In China, people are still judged by their looks, education, nationality, sexuality, and wealth; immigrants still struggle to assimilate to cultural ideals they can't quite attain, and for which they're socially punished when they fail. Convicts may now be sent to colonize Mars instead of to prison, but in *China Mountain Zhang* the poor are still targeted by police. Capitalism has failed residents of the neoliberal West, but communism offers nothing better, largely because both economic systems play by the same rules around identity when it comes to ideas about success. Neither political system takes care of "people in the cracks," since both require upholding the fantasy of the ideal citizen—the "model minority"—to pit different communities against each other so as to protect the state's authority. Thus the Chinese have become "the worst racists in the world," as one character complains, not because they are by nature more racist but because the racism they promote serves the interest of institutional dominance.

It doesn't take much sleuthing to see that McHugh's novel is as much about late-twentieth-century America as it is about China, and that Zhang's transformations throughout the novel are there to prove how finally arbitrary are any "standards" a nation promotes to maintain racial and sexual distinctions. Even though he's bio-logically half-Chinese and (through surgery) completely Chinese in his appearance, Zhang is constantly accused of being "not Chinese enough" because he's American-born, because he's poor, because he has an accent, because he isn't straight. Even as he succeeds at his job, Zhang continues to fail at being seen as a man. In that sense, McHugh's novel reminds me that race, sexuality, and gender are fluid constructions that are both self- and socially imposed.

But the final reason the novel feels truthful to me is because, at heart, it's the classic immigrant's tale, with a twist. When Zhang, taught from birth to idolize China, discovers that he can't hide his true and complex identities in "the motherland," he rejects assimilation and returns to New York and the lure of becoming something more conceptually slippery, a transnational, transcultural figure who doesn't merely "survive between the cracks" but is only "free when [he] slip[s] between the cracks." For Zhang, these "cracks" release him from the particular burden of having to fit in anywhere. With *China Mountain Zhang*, McHugh has not only understood something very true about how we teach ourselves to categorize and imagine identity, she has understood—whether accidentally or deliberately—something fundamental about the Asian American literary tradition and its reinvention of the immigration narrative.

Did McHugh get being Chinese entirely "right" in her cultural references and in her use of Chinese dialogue that peppers the novel? Probably not. But I believe she understands how "Chinese" and "American" and "straight" and "gay" get categorically constructed and deconstructed. She doesn't make certain characters perform my ideas of their otherness; instead, she shows me how *everyone* is forced to perform their identities in a world that literally constructs and capitalizes upon difference.

APPROPRIATING WHITENESS

As I write this, it strikes me that many of the most compelling examples of appropriation I've included in these letters so far were written by a mixed-race man and White women. Perhaps you recognize that these identities have a strong sense of Du Bois's double consciousness drilled into them from an early age, too, and so perhaps all underrepresented identities have a psychological edge when it comes to writing in the voice of others. So should you and I only be worried about appropriative works authored by White men? Can writers of color appropriate White subjects in ways that are racist?

If I assume that a writer of color is more familiar with other people of color and Eurocentric cultures than White writers are, perhaps I might extend this assumption to say that the person of color can write from the perspective of *any* underrepresented position, as if all raced, gendered, ability, and class positions were the same. There are two problems with this, however, one being that while underrepresented people in America may share similar insights into the experience of being "othered," they don't share all the same insights or experiences. Though I myself have experienced Du Bois's double consciousness, I don't know what it means to be Black, or gay, or disabled. I have experienced prejudice particular to *my* bodily difference, not everyone's. The second problem is that, by my placing all non-majority identities into the same category, I reify the monolithic status the majority holds. I implicitly make the default identity position White, male, middle-class, and able-bodied.

The question, X, is whether certain identities are absolved from holding racist ideas about other people, or even about themselves. But as Ibram X. Kendi reminds us in *How to Be an Antiracist*, racist ideas are those that "suggest one racial group is superior or inferior to another racial group in any way." If racism in literature relies upon the consistent use of negative metaphors to depict racial hierarchies, then anyone who employs these metaphors expresses a racist idea, regardless of her own identity. In that, White people are not the only ones who can express racist ideas, just as men are not the only ones who can express misogynist ideas. Black people can express racist ideas, about other Blacks, Latinx people, Asians, and also White people. The question, however, is whether these portrayals carry the same social and historical weight in our literature, and whether these racist ideas translate to policies that affect our institutions.

Personally, I would hope that anyone who wants to challenge racist thinking would reject racist ideas of any kind, but I understand that many of our institutions are still shaped by policies that privilege White people. In that, the racist ideas expressed by people of color do not culturally hold as much weight as those expressed by White people, in part because our institutions are still predominantly White, and because of the sheer number of positive representations we have of White people—on our televisions, on our movie screens, in our poems and in our fiction. Frankly, X, White people can survive a little bad press, and they certainly have the cultural capital to put out more good press of their own.

But while writers of color might express racist ideas about other groups, I do believe they have a distinct edge in imagining Eurocentric cultures. In part, this is because of the historical predominance of White male characters in literature, which has required non-White and female readers to imaginatively inhabit protagonists who do not share their identity. One of my favorite books as a teen was *A Separate Peace*, not because I saw my world at all reflected in the tony microcosm of Phillips Exeter Academy, but because I identified my own sense of being an outsider inside of Gene Forrester's sensitivity, his heart-catching lack of social grace. When it comes to approximating White men on the page, X, it's easy for me to slip outside my consciousness since I've been studying for years men's particular shyness, envies, and swagger.

As to people of color writing from the perspective of White people, interestingly, Du Bois, in his 1920 book *Darkness*, included a chapter called "The Souls of White Folk" in which he calls Black Americans' specific ability to see, and see through, the psyches of White Americans a kind of "clairvoyance"—one that allows them to see their tormentors more clearly than they can see themselves, and thus protect them from the deceptions of what he terms "the religion of whiteness." Du Bois writes, "We, whose shame, humiliation and deep insult [the white man's] aggrandizement so often involved were never deceived. We looked at him clearly, with old-world eyes, and saw simply a human thing, weak and pitiable and cruel, even as we were and are." When Du Bois suggests that African Americans are more capable of seeing White Americans than the reverse because White Americans can only see African Americans through the lens of racial prejudice, he's also arguing that African Americans—as a method of both psychic and physical survival—must learn to separate themselves from their stereotypes to accurately read the social intentions of Whites. Black clairvoyance would have, I believe, literary effects as well, since it allows Black writers to better "see" from a White perspective.

I was thinking about Du Bois and Whiteness recently while rereading Patricia Smith's famous 1992 persona poem "Skinhead," which displays a concise understanding of the racial, economic, and sexual politics that construct White masculinity. It's an understanding that verges at times on something like sympathy for the speaker's masochism, even if Skinhead himself would reject anyone's sympathy. In "Skinhead," the speaker unveils himself to us through images of his body, which is wounded both by his own actions and by the general indifference of the world to his "own beauty," as the speaker calls it, even as he admits that his face is "huge and pockmarked / scraped pink . . . [and] filled with [his] own spit." Smith's speaker is identified by his racist beliefs, naming himself "Skinhead" because it's the term "knife-scrawled across [his] back in sore, jagged letters." Skinhead "sits in [his] dim matchbox" of a room and

> [s]lide[s] razors across [his] hair,
> count[s] how many ways
> [he] can bring blood closer to the surface of [his] skin.

Skinhead's fascination with pain is both, he says, a "dut[y] of the righteous" but also a way of drawing my attention to his physicality. Of course, if racism depends upon appearance, it makes sense that Skinhead is obsessed with his flesh; blood for him is not only the evidence of pain but of race, and Whiteness and pain for Skinhead are merged throughout the poem. Skinhead repeatedly acknowledges he's not a successful or particularly beautiful example of his race, his own hand ruined from when "a machine that slices leather / whack[ed] off three fingers at the root," leading to the loss of his job and a mutilated hand with "only the baby finger left, sticking straight up." In Smith's poem, Skinhead's hand becomes a symbol of his emasculation, as it leaves him both unable to work and unable to offer a proper "fuck you" to those who look at him as "some kind of freak," because the pinky finger is of course "the wrong goddamned finger," as Skinhead himself knows.

Skinhead's emasculation is only reinforced when he sees working African American and Chicano men "walking like kings up and down the sidewalks in my head / walking like their fat black mamas *named* them freedom." His envy of their confidence mixes with disgust for his own appearance, driving him toward grotesque acts of violence in which he can transfer his own masochistic tendencies onto the bodies of men of color.

"It's a kick to watch their eyes get big," he writes of his attacks, "right in that second when they know the pipe's gonna come down." If we read Skinhead's "baby finger" as his unsatisfactory phallic symbol, the metal pipe he uses to beat black and Chicano men becomes its grotesque replacement, something Smith suggests in the fact that Skinhead gets an erection during his violence. "I get hard," he says, "listening to their skin burst." Skinhead's racism is a combustible brew of self-hatred, envy, economic disappointment, and homoeroticism—all things he can name but can't consider because he believes the cause of his rage is external. He won't acknowledge that the systems of racial power he supports have made him as vulnerable as they have people of color, and he can't imagine he won't reap the rewards Whiteness should pay.

Skinhead's refusal to believe in his own failure makes the end of the poem both terrifying and strangely triumphal. "I'm riding the top rung of the perfect race," Skinhead crows, and regardless of how much I might want to see Skinhead as an American aberration who's perverted our values, Skinhead insists he's central to the American narrative. "I'm your baby, America," he spits,

> your boy . . . And I was born
> and raised
> right here.

Skinhead's rhetoric and self-justification may at times read as reductive, but racist ideas are themselves reductive: certain bodies must reflect specific values in order for them to preserve their racial meanings. It's why Skinhead's obsession with his body becomes so important. Stripped of his job, his physical wholeness, his sense of self and future, Skinhead has nothing but skin color to suggest his superiority. Skinhead possesses the *physical* fact of Whiteness, but none of what he thinks its social, sexual, and economic advantages are.

Smith's poem is at once a very direct and psychologically complex examination of White, working-class masculinity, and its popularity is due in part to Smith having performed it on *Def Jam Poets*, a performance that one of my poetry students reminded me was a sly dig at slam monologues popular during the '90s. At the time, these monologues tended more toward the autobiographical than the invented persona, especially toward monologues that celebrated the poet's triumph over prejudice, something Smith—one of America's premier performance poets—would certainly know. To have a Black woman performing the voice of a White working-class skinhead in a space that prioritizes the triumphal autobiographical narrative would be a comment on conventional audience expectations. And by watching—not just reading—Smith's poem, I have to see Skinhead translated through her own Black, female body. By listening to her in a space where the audience roots for those who suffer under a racist ideology, I have to check my impulse to applaud all self-revelation, and also to expand my understanding of whom racism affects. I have to imagine how racist ideology harms both people of color *and* working-class Whites.

Smith's poem—both in its writing and its performance—understands the intertwined ways in which race gets constructed, imagined, read over, and translated. Racial identity is not, as Skinhead believes, simply determined by one's skin color but by one's gender, one's economic position, even by one's relationship to other people's genders and economic positions. As Smith reminds us, Whiteness, too, is constantly in flux, a relation and not a static proposition.

Other poets of color have, like Smith, written powerful persona poems outside their identity positions, and one of the most famous was Ai, whose book *Killing Floor* shot her to national fame in 1978. In the book's title poem, Ai, a mixed-race woman of Japanese, Choctaw-Chickasaw, African American, Irish, Southern Cheyenne, and Comanche descent, writes from the perspective of Leon Trotsky, the Russian and Jewish revolutionary, Marxist theorist, and Soviet politician. Trotsky was murdered in 1940 in Mexico by an agent of Stalin whom Trotsky philosophically and politically opposed, a fact the poem references by its end, though it opens in 1927 in Russia, with Trotsky being pushed into a river by a "sienna-skinned man" with "spade-shaped hands." Here is the poem's first stanza:

On the day the sienna-skinned man
held my shoulders between his spade-shaped hands,
easing me down into the azure water of Jordan,
I woke ninety-three million miles from myself,

Lev Davidovich Bronstein,

shoulder-deep in the Volga,

while the cheap dye of my black silk shirt darkened the water.

The phrase "spade-shaped hands" is meant to recall the ice ax that Jacques uses to murder Trotsky with later, both in life and in the poem, and so from its beginning, the poem casts Trotsky as a man marked for death. Trotsky reminds the reader of his original, forgotten name, Lev Davidovich Bronstein, even as he also imagines "[waking] ninety-three million miles" from himself; in that, Trotsky as we know him is thus both present and absent in the poem, someone who shifts and changes as the poem unfolds. Even the river in which he's being dunked isn't a stable location: it's either "the azure waters of Jordan" or the Russian Volga, whose waters darken with the "cheap dye of [his] black silk shirt."

For me, that image of dye darkening the water both anticipates the bloodstains from Trotsky's murder, and echoes the blurriness of Trotsky's own ethnic identity in the poem, the sense of Trotsky himself bleeding out of his own boundaries. This, too, is echoed by Trotsky's question to himself in the second stanza, as he tries to blink water out of his lashes: "Am I blind?" he asks himself. This question is never answered, just as Trotsky can't answer Stalin's question in the poem about what he saw in the river, outside of recounting an image of

a man drowning in water and holiness,

the castrati voices I can't recognize,

skating on knives, from trees, from air

on the thin ice of my last night in Russia.

Leon Trotsky. Bread.

I want to scream, but silence holds my tongue
with small spade-shaped hands
and only this comes, so quietly
Stalin has to press his ear to my mouth:
I have only myself. Put me on the train.
I won't look back.

"I have only myself" is an ironic line, since not only will Trotsky soon be murdered, I have very little sense of who Trotsky—or anyone else in the poem—actually is. That lack of clarity is, I think, important. The poem is structured by associative, symbolic repetition, not plot-driven narrative that suggests cause and effect, as well as an unfolding sense of time. Occasionally, Ai employs hypotactic sentence structures that bury the main clause; at other times, she juts fragments against each other without any clear subordination, so that identities, objects and even events become equivalent. "Leon Trotsky. Bread," she writes, as if the two things shared the same importance. Ai's syntax and lineation encourage me to lose track of her primary subject, just as Trotsky loses track of his own history. Essentially, Ai has written a persona poem in the voice of a man who has no specific identity.

If you read Ai's long body of work, you'll see that she writes persona poems in the voice of Oppenheimer, Joseph McCarthy, a leftist soldier dying in the Spanish Civil War, the 1981 Atlanta child killer, and an aging journalist recalling Vietnam: essentially almost any major public figure in personal or historical crisis. If there's one desire that motivates Ai's poems, it's the desire to look beyond violent events into the psychology of those who effect or who are affected by violence. In the case of "Killing Floor," it's the essential slipperiness of an assassinated man's identity. In the case of "Testimony of J. Robert Oppenheimer," however, it's the application of atomic theory to Oppenheimer's belief that humanity will destroy itself, a return to nothingness that is like being "born again and again / from that dark, metal womb" of nuclear destruction, where

> [w]e strip away the tattered fabric
> of the universe
> to the juicy, dark meat,
> the nothing beyond time.
> We tear ourselves down atom by atom,
> till electron and positron,
> we become our own transcendent annihilation.

Ai never purports to depict these men as themselves or to speak for them, but to speak *about* them in the language and symbols you and I already associate with them; in that way, she can reveal some truth about their inner voice. If Trotsky becomes an icon, a martyr, and a cipher, notice how Ai applies religious and dreamlike imagery to his constantly shifting identity. If Oppenheimer is, for general readers, forever linked to the atomic bomb, notice how she uses atomic rhetoric and imagery to filter his own sense of the world. Ai isn't interested in getting these men "right" according to how they might have been in real life, but accurate to a larger truth of how we have historically imagined them. It's why the poems don't read as appropriations of an individual's life and private experience, because in essence we have all shared in the creation of these lives and experiences.

That's not to say that these personas don't read as "real" men: they, like any actual person, experience vivid dreams, physical sensations, and fears. They're certainly not caricatures whose interior lives are *only* defined by their historical actions. But they explain their actions in the language and imagery I've come to expect with them, which is why their monologues feel believable to me. These poems speak to me as much about my historical fantasies as their own biographical details, and it's that mixture of the socially constructed and the individually imagined identity, that conflict between the public and the private life, that is the real subject of Ai's monologues.

RACE AS ACTIVE METAPHOR

I recognize that, when talking about Ai's poems, I'm arguing for something that directly contradicts what I wrote you before about *Nat Turner*'s reception, which is that to make a portrayal of a real character believable you might depict him in imagery your audience will recognize. If that's the case, aren't I then arguing for us to reduce people to metaphors? Well, yes and no. I believe you can figure someone metaphorically without reducing him to a negative stereotype. In Viet Thanh Nguyen's *The Sympathizer*, for example, the protagonist is a half-French, half-Vietnamese captain in the South Vietnamese Army who's also a spy for the North. From the start of the novel, the narrator is described as "a spy, a sleeper, a spook, a man of two faces." Obviously, Nguyen has made this character's race have figurative meanings. Like Vietnam itself, the protagonist is politically, culturally, and historically divided, divisions that only create more conflict in the speaker once he emigrates to the United States. His loyalty, like his mixed identity, is constantly in question. But the very complexity of the protagonist's identity means I cannot assign him only one racial value or attitude; as soon as I see how his identity might be shaped one way, changed circumstances encourage him to act another. If the metaphor for being biracial is multiplicity and contradiction, the novel sustains that metaphor. But this metaphor also allows the protagonist to express a range of feelings and behaviors that, finally, cannot only be attached to the character's biracialism without making the novel reductive.

Nguyen's approach stands in stark contrast to the way that Chang Rae Lee's *Native Speaker* uses the metaphor of biracialism. In *Native Speaker*, the Korean American protagonist Henry Park (also, interestingly, a spy with complicated allegiances) has a mixed-race child named Mitt with his White wife, Lelia. Mitt dies in an accident, and the conversation Lelia and Henry have after their son's death reveals the profound ambivalence both Lelia and Henry have about Mitt, and about their mixed marriage. As Lelia says,

> When your baby dies it's never an accident . . . Sometimes I think it's more like some long-turning karma that finally came back for us . . . Maybe it's that Mitt wasn't all white or all yellow. I go crazy thinking about it. Don't you? Maybe the world wasn't ready for him.

As with Nguyen's protagonist, Lee has made the child's mixed-race background a metaphor for cultural confusion, though in this case it's not the child's confusion but Henry's and Lelia's. Henry's son dies for many of the same reasons so many mixed-race characters die or commit suicide in novels such as *Uncle Tom's Cabin* or *Passing*: Mitt is a Tragic Mulatto archetype, because in a world divided into strict racial categories, the child of miscegenation cannot exist.

Am I, a biracial person, offended by Lee's use of the Tragic

Mulatto figure? No. But I see it for what it is, and I recognize that what I'm encountering is not a character but a plot device.

The fact is, some metaphors offer the reader more nuance and complexity than others when it comes to depicting people on the page, because some metaphors do not substantiate racist hierarchies and meanings even as they may recognize racial difference. For example, Ralph Ellison's unnamed Black protagonist in *Invisible Man* lives in an underground room filled with lights whose electric power he's siphoned off the city's grid. Clearly, the narrator's living space is a metaphor for the speaker's race, in particular the ways in which Black identity becomes invisible to White Americans who refuse to see African Americans. But it's also a metaphor for Black resistance and survival, too, for how it might quietly undermine the very power structures that erase him, and by doing so allow the individual to see himself more clearly, apart from the world that would shunt him to the margins.

In a way, what makes these racial metaphors rise above archetypes is that they don't tell us about how to read racial identity *as itself*, but how to read the society that constructs racial identity. They don't assign their characters only one possible meaning, which I think you see in Hemingway's depiction of Native suicide in "Indian Camp." Expansive and not reductive racial metaphors point outward, not inward. I don't read *Invisible Man* or *The Sympathizer* believing that these metaphors will tell me something only and unalterably true about these particular racialized identities, but to understand how these racial identities must literally and figuratively function in spaces that think in Black and White.

Because here's what makes the race-as-metaphor problem difficult, X: The fact is, I *do* understand that my racial identity has figurative as well as literal meanings. I, too, have used biracial identity in my writing as a metaphor for being cognitively divided. My experience of being alive has been, at times, one of great contradiction and pain, as my identity in America is both seen and unseen, present and absent, native and foreign all at once. Perhaps that's why I don't mind Nguyen's rendition of biracial identity—an identity, notably, he himself does not share—because it realizes something true about racial difference that is also psychologically true for me. Nguyen's metaphor embroiders upon one aspect of my identity while also allowing for the radical recognition of what constitutes some part of my "otherness" for the reader.

The distinction I'm making is subtle, but it's also the paradoxical heart of good writing, which shapes characters from figurative generalities while also resisting stereotypes or caricature. Writing expands upon and shrinks reality at once. As a writer, I know that our characterizations of other people are gestural approximations of what we ourselves have experienced or seen others endure, and the more our portraits have metaphorical resonance within the story we're telling, the more they make the work as a whole come alive.

Which is again why writing risks being transgressive, whether or not we write in the voices of others. Writers take and remake everything we see around us: we metabolize the details of our loved ones, alter time and memory, shapeshift our personal and physical differences into transformative images that, when done with care, can create a world that feels more than accurate, but real. Doing this requires that we watch and listen to one another with great attention, something we're generally discouraged from doing lest we come off as stalkers. From the time we're children, we're taught it's rude to stare, nosy to eavesdrop; you can't just root around in other people's journals and closets and minds. I can't ask my colleagues what they *really* think and feel about their marriages or children, because that's private, and privacy requires that I pretend to believe what both strangers and loved ones tell me. Being polite means, ironically, paying *less* attention to the people I want to be close to, bypassing their foibles and idiosyncrasies and quiet outrages in the name of communal goodwill. But writing requires we pay attention to others at a level that can only be classified as rude. The writer sees the button trailing by its single thread on the pastor's shirt; she tastes the acid sting behind a mother's compliment. To observe closely leads the writer to the radical recognition of what both binds her to and separates her from others. It will push her to hear voices she's been taught should remain silent. Oftentimes, these voices, and these truths, reveal something equally powerful, and profoundly unsettling, about ourselves.

I want to end this letter to you by proposing something that some critics and sociologists might reject out of hand, which is the possibility that White people, too, might, by paying close attention to the voices around them and inside themselves, be able to experience double consciousness. If double consciousness is in part based on the understanding of the systemic power of Whiteness, and if it is also the realization that one's self-regard can never be divorced from the gaze of others, then the practice of double consciousness might be available to everyone, including those who constitute the majority.

I say "practice" because I don't think this is going to be something that comes to many people without effort. In general, White people do not have to struggle to separate their self-perception from pervasive negative stereotypes of them that are widely and historically held, and also institutionally enforced. I think double consciousness is something some of us must be trained into experiencing, much in the ways that we have each learned—and continue to learn—what constitutes privilege, and how widespread and automatic racist thinking is. But I also think that Whiteness is itself a fraught identity that contains multitudes, paradoxes, and inherent conflicts. It is, historically, an identity that's been both phenomenally flexible and rigid in its application, even as it has been relentlessly policed by those from within. Whiteness, as much as any other racial category, has been open to dispute even if it has not been widely subject to persecution; it has historically been tied to class, labor, political power, geography and even sexual preference; it has been treated as something that might be earned through work, education, and through intermarriage, and in that, Whiteness is always framed by the gaze of the non-White.

Whiteness, I have also personally learned, is something that might even be imposed upon you by those uncomfortable with the specter of the non-White. If the White writer was to look at her race in much the same way she's trained to look at non-White identity—as a series of choices and behaviors that are reinforced by her daily encounters in the world—she might quickly recognize how much these "definitions" don't actually apply to her, even if she benefits from them. She would feel the split in her identity between how she is perceived and what she is. She might even begin to reject what Whiteness is and represents.

Perhaps, however, this is not experiencing Du Bois's double consciousness so much as becoming conscious about what it means to be raced at all. In any case, such consciousness can only help you if you are intent on representing the experience of someone unlike yourself. If you can't be so easily encapsulated, why should anyone else be? To understand that we are each—at best—a set of relations and possibilities, not inevitabilities, is a great lesson to be learned. It may not make your representations absolutely accurate, X, but it will help make your performances on the page more convincing when you learn how to start seeing others, while listening to what they have to say.

LETTER FIVE

Appropriation as Racial Hoax

Dear X:

In 2015, *The Best American Poetry* series anthology included a poem titled "The Bees, The Flowers, Jesus, Ancient Tigers, Poseidon, Adam and Eve." Perhaps you remember this poem, in particular the fact that it was authored by a White, male poet named Michael Derrick Hudson who published it under the name Yi-Fen Chou, the pseudonym Hudson used to get the poem taken by the literary magazine *Prairie Schooner*, which *The Best American Poetry* guest editor at the time, Sherman Alexie, then happened upon. Hudson confessed his true identity to Alexie after he learned of his poem's anthology selection; he also confessed his use of the female Chinese pseudonym in the final published anthology's biographical notes. Hudson wrote that he'd chosen the name only after the poem had been rejected forty times by different journals. The female Chinese name,

Hudson's note implied, made a previously unpublishable poem suddenly attractive.

You can imagine how Hudson's appropriation of this name—one, it was later uncovered, that belonged to an *actual* former female high-school classmate of Hudson's—caused outrage among Asian American writers, many who've seen themselves passed over by such prestigious publications as *Best American Poetry*. Their anger only increased when readers and critics argued in defense of Hudson that, as race itself was merely a social construct, it might be effectively explored through false personas, an argument that I think is a pretty obtuse diminishment of both Asian American writers and our lived experiences in the world.

I began these letters to you, X, with the working assumption that you, like most writers, are concerned about how and if to write about the lives of others through their fictionalized voices. I believe you're concerned about the ethical risk in appropriative works the reader understands to be imaginative. I assume you are *not* planning the far more radical proposition of pretending *to be* another person through your work, even though literary history is filled with people who've created raced or underrepresented personas for themselves, or who've passed their work off as genuine expressions of events and lives. Such hoaxes and fakes pop up with surprising regularity. There are fake slave narratives and bogus indigenous oral histories, there is Nasdijj and Grey Owl and *The Education of Little Tree*, there is James Frey's fictitious imprisonment in *A Million Little Pieces*, there is the debunked *Misha: A Memoire of the Holocaust Years*, and, most recently, there is the Canadian writer Joseph Boyden, who falsely claimed to be Métis.

But though you may not be planning to take on such a false identity, X, I want to explain to you just why such racial fakes are painful.

I came across my own first hoax in an Asian American Poetry class I taught fifteen years ago at my university. The fake was named Charles Yu, and his poems were included in our class-assigned anthology of Asian American poetry from the late nineteenth century up to the 1970s entitled *Quiet Fire*. According to the anthology's biography, Charles Yu was a Chinese student living in Chicago in the late 1930s; after a random Internet search, however, I discovered through a rare bookseller's site that Yu was actually the pseudonym for a Jewish American editor for G. P. Putnam's Sons named William Targ: interestingly, the same editor who rose to national prominence for buying and editing the *Godfather* novels. In 1941, Black Archer Press brought out Targ's *Poems of a Chinese Student* under Yu's name after several poems were published in the *Chicago Tribune*.

The students in my class, to my chagrin, were ecstatic. All semester long I'd fielded questions from a small but vocal minority of students resistant to taking my class in order to fulfill the university's diversity requirement. Over several weeks these students questioned my course's relevance to English literature, increasing my own concerns about this subject which meant, personally, so much to me but which seemed to have so few dedicated Asian American poetry anthologies for the field. *Quiet Fire* was the only historical overview of its kind I could find; frankly, I hated it. So many of the poems insulted my intelligence about racial politics in America, and they offered little opportunity for in-depth analysis for the students. I had chosen the anthology the way some of my students had chosen my course—based on market constraints and artificial requirements— and so each night before class, I'd sit at my desk, groaning as I tried to imagine how I would fake fresh enthusiasm for my detractors who sat at the back of class, glaring into their dog-eared books. For a while, I even toyed with the idea of pretending to be White for the semester in the vague, self-hating hopes that my presumed Whiteness might validate the subject where my Asianness would only further undercut it.

"What's the point of segregating literature unless the poems can't hold up?" one student argued the day before midterms, holding up *Quiet Fire* with the tips of his fingers. "If it's good literature, then we should just read it all together."

"An excellent suggestion," I replied. "One I'm sure our university has already taken. So how many great poems that happen to have been written by Asian Americans have you read in your literature courses?" The students looked baffled. "African Americans?" A few shrugged. "Latinos?" They glanced at each other.

"Well," one student finally said. "*None*, of course."

It was that "of course" that came ringing back to my ears upon the discovery of Charles Yu. Here it was at last, X, proof for my students that race was little more than a formulaic narrative anyone could forge. The fact that an Asian American professor had fallen for the hoax itself proved I had never been interested in literature but representation. Who knew how many other writers weren't actually Asian American or African American or Latinx in these anthologies they were now being forced to purchase; who knew how many other, better, White writers were being ignored at the expense of politics?

Rightly or wrongly, X, their resentment throughout that semester stung. It made me feel responsible both for Yu and for the university's diversity requirement. Targ's fake meant I had a literature now as well as an identity to defend.

Of course, if you read the poems of "Charles Yu" closely today, you'll see how little Targ did to hide his identity. Targ used the Yu poems to satirize and celebrate the idea of America as a racial melt-

ing pot, not really to imagine being Chinese. In his poem, "In America," for example, Yu and his friend (a mysterious Miss Jones) enter
a nightclub to find "a beautiful Negress" standing onstage, singing a
Yiddish lament. The poem swiftly descends into an Orientalist fan-
tasia of racial mixing in which the "exotic" sexuality of the Black
singer is exaggerated. Her skin, Yu notes, is "brown as fresh iodine, /
her lips [like] coral lacquer"; she fills the entire club with "the quick-
ening scent of [her] musk" while singing to "the beat of a tom-tom."
It's a poem that lampoons race, a fact Targ also seems aware of, as he
outs himself as its author in the final stanza:

> Only in America could it occur:
> This Negress passionately singing
> *Eli Eli Lomo Asovtoni*,
> The Yiddish lament
> Written by a New Yorker
> For a drama dealing
> With Chinese Jews.

Chinese Jews? Clearly, Targ was trying to let his audience in on the
joke. I understand the likely reason Targ's work had been included
in *Quiet Fire* was that there's a dearth of Asian American poetry
written in English in the early part of the twentieth century. But the
existence of such a fake in this anthology—one edited by an Asian
American editor, no less—spurred me to seek out other such hoaxes.
I wanted to find in these fakes a key to their mistaken racial logic, a
flaw I might pinpoint to determine that there *was* in fact something
authentic about being Chinese, or Asian, or Asian American, something that could not be faked, whose absence would be glaring to the

Asian reader. But what if I found a fake that, aesthetically, I liked or that convinced me of its authenticity? What would that mean about me as a reader, and as an Asian American? What if my students, even if they expressed ideas about literature that I recognized were racist, were also somehow right? And that's how I discovered Araki Yasusada.

ARAKI YASUSADA AND THE POLITICS OF RACIAL FAKES

Around the mid-1980s, a number of poems began appearing in American literary journals under the name Araki Yasusada. According to his biography, Araki Yasusada was a relatively unknown and deceased Japanese poet who'd survived the bombing of Hiroshima but who lost almost his entire family in the blast. An avid reader of Jack Spicer and Roland Barthes, Yasusada had sporadically published his poems in Japanese avant-garde literary magazines, becoming famous to American readers only after English translations of his work surfaced in the pages of journals like *The American Poetry Review*, *Grand Street*, and *Conjunctions*. Readers and critics, entranced by the poems, clamored for more except, oddly, no one seemed able to reach Yasusada's estate. Kent Johnson, a poet, community college teacher, and translator of Spanish poetry, was Yasusada's purported contact, and it was he who sent Yasusada's poems off for publication. Rumors that Yasusada had never existed soon began to surface, and Wesleyan University Press, which had first offered to publish a volume of Yasusada's work, quietly withdrew its contract.

All this, however, didn't stop American interest in Araki Yasusada. If anything, it made his work an underground sensation, and

Doubled Flowering: From the Notebooks of Araki Yasusada, the only available book of his poetry to date, was later published by Roof Books in 1997. So far, no one has come forward to claim responsibility for the hoax, though its author is almost certainly Kent Johnson, the poet who sent Yasusada's work to magazines on behalf of Yasusada's "translators," and who edited *Doubled Flowering*. Johnson, at least, is the one to whom all the literary journals' fee checks were written.

The Yi-Fen Chou and Charles Yu scandals are strange, X, but you can see that there's a whole new level of insanity to Araki Yasusada, in part because of the different levels of seriousness to the poets' biographies, in part because of the authors' differing commitments to their frauds. It's one thing to pretend to be a Chinese student living in Chicago in the 1930s or to occasionally publish a poem under another person's name. It's another thing entirely to pretend having survived the bombing of Hiroshima, to claim you've lost your wife and youngest daughter in the blast, and to describe watching your eldest daughter perish of radiation sickness four years later.

For Targ and Hudson, their authors' racial identities are almost beside the point. The Chou and Yu poems aren't interested in discovering what it means to be Chinese or Chinese American, because they are personas or pseudonyms through which their authors can either get published or, in Targ's case, parody multiculturalism. If you read Hudson's "The Bees, The Flowers, Jesus, Ancient Tigers, Poseidon, Adam and Eve" (a title that accurately sums up everything that appears in the poem) you'll discover there's no reason for Hudson to have chosen a Chinese name at all, since the poem makes no reference to any specific information about race or culture, though certain readers might make much of lines like the following:

Am I supposed to say something, add
a soundtrack and voiceover? My life's spent

running an inept tour for my own sad swindle of a vacation

until every goddamned thing's reduced to botched captions
and dabs of misinformation in fractured,

not-quite-right English . . .

Much, that is, if you want to find Hudson's admission to being "the voiceover" buried within these lines or see the phrase "fractured, // not-quite-right English" as a racist nod to the identity he's appropriated. But if Hudson just wanted to plump his CV, Targ's point was to play a joke on his audience, a theory proven by the fact he once appeared at a Chicago book club that invited "Charles Yu" to read his poems, and he also outs himself as Yu in his memoir, *Indecent Pleasures*.

In this, Hudson and Targ are fundamentally different from Yasusada, who never reveals his true identity. Indeed, Yasusada is in fact a persona within a persona, since Johnson now insists it's another Japanese poet, Tosa Motakiyu, who was the one to invent him and who has now, rather conveniently, died.

But the fact Johnson insists upon the existence of Motakiyu at all is telling; at first, I read the Yasusada project as one of imaginative empathy, something Lionel Shriver herself might approve of, and it's become one of the longest-running attempts to fake a persona that American readers might treat as authentic. Thus the letters, the fragments, the rough drafts and translator's notes, even the shopping lists scattered throughout *Doubled Flowering*: I can see that Johnson has assembled a world from these quotidian scraps he's imagined to prove a life is at stake, a life based upon experience, violence, art, and history. Implicitly, Johnson is arguing that a specific cultural identity *can* imaginatively be created, and that autobiographical experience, or authentic national citizenship, aren't prerequisites for the making of transcultural art.

With the Yasusada poems, the question of race and ethnicity are profoundly important to consider, because while I might focus on Yasusada's nationality as the appropriated identity, here national boundaries also represent racial ones. Japanese racial difference is certainly one of the factors that influenced how the United States treated its Japanese American residents and citizens during the war, and how it also decided in favor of dropping nuclear bombs on Japan. Perhaps, however, you think the worst thing Johnson appropriated was Yasusada's personal experience: Yasusada offends because his identity as a *war victim* is fake. Still, I would argue that we must take race into consideration, as at times the poems in *Doubled Flowering* demand that I equate Yasusada's experience as a war victim with his also being racially Japanese. I can see this in his poem "Walkers with Ladle," in which a mysterious group of people Yasusada simply refers to as "they" command the poet, in English, "Don't you dare fucking walk you fucking Jap fucker." For me, these interconnected national, racial, and traumatized identities contained within Yasusada are what make the hoax so fascinating, and a more complex form of appropriation than either Targ's or Hudson's poems.

Finally, the Yasusada poems are different from Targ's and Hudson's by the simple fact that they are, aesthetically, more sophisticated. Frankly, X, I liked Yasusada's poems. And considering what I wrote you before about there being no unbreakable link between race and the cultural products artists can produce, I have to take my aesthetic pleasure in Yasusada with unnerving seriousness; that is, I have to ask myself whether there's some larger value to these poems, regardless of Yasusada's actual identity. When I presented Yasusada's work to my class, my gut desire was to reject the poems outright, but the commitment to the fake, the sheer amount of writing "Yasusada" produced, suggests that there's more psychologically at stake for Johnson. If I'm supposed to read these poems as an American elegy for the bombings in Hiroshima and Nagasaki, for the racist acts America committed against the Japanese on its own soil, then perhaps the fact that Johnson refuses to identify himself as the author implies that, to him, Yasusada *does* exist, if not in a Japanese poetic imagination, then in an American one. Johnson's silence might, then, suggest that Americans are the ones who need Yasusada to be real, to explain and perhaps be forgiven (by ourselves, ironically) for the bombings in the war.

But before I consider whether or not the poems are an apology, I want to spend time thinking about why I found the poems so appealing to begin with, especially those whose subject matter were most closely, if elliptically, tied to the poet's biography. Poems like "Telescope with Urn," "Trolley Fare and Blossom," and "Mad Daughter and Big-Bang" I found surprisingly moving, considering how they evoked personal pain without giving in to autobiographical detail or actual sentiment. For me, they suggested rather than declaimed the horrors of Hiroshima, placing me on the margins of the poem while focusing my attention instead on the poem's surreal style. "Mad Daughter and Big-Bang" might be the most successful example of this suppression of the autobiographical in service to the surreal, and it's the one I found most haunting. Here is the poem in its entirety:

Walking in the vegetable patch
late at night, I was startled to find
the severed head of my
mad daughter lying on the ground.

Her eyes were upturned, gazing at me, ecstatic-like . . .

(from a distance it had appeared to be a stone, haloed with light,
as if cast there by the Big-Bang.)

What on earth are you doing, I said,
you look ridiculous.

Some boys buried me here,
she said sullenly.

Her dark hair, comet-like, trailed behind . . .

Squatting, I pulled the
turnip by the root.

From its start, the poem relies upon the distressing "facts" of Yasusa-da's biography, beginning with the disturbing image of the narrator, a father, finding the decapitated head of his daughter in a vegetable patch, "[h]er eyes . . . upturned, gazing at [him] ecstatic-like." It then jumps to a parenthetical description of the atomic bomb detonating over the city, its explosion like "a stone, haloed with light, / as if cast there by the Big-Bang." When the poet asks his daughter's head what it's doing on the ground, the head replies "sullenly" that some boys buried it there, and the poet, squatting, pulls a "turnip by the root."

These disjunctive images may feel arbitrary, but the poem soon unfolds into a coherent biography of the bomb's impact on Yasusada's family. Images of the universe's origin repeat in the poem, appearing in reference to the bomb that leveled Hiroshima, but also in the narrator's description of his daughter's hair which "[trails], comet-like" behind her head. The image of the turnip at the poem's end resonates with the image of the mad daughter's head, implying the daughter has been killed by the bomb, and by those "boys" who initiated the war. Indeed, the war's effects continue to haunt her: the daughter seems to gaze ecstatically at both the narrator and the bomb, awed by its half-divine, half-natural force.

What strikes me about the poem, X, is how naturally the sublime moves into the absurd, the grotesque, the cruel. After the description of the bombing, for example, Yasusada tells his daughter that she looks "ridiculous" with her head in the ground, as if attempting to dismiss the shock of her death. And while the daughter's face and hair are described with great tenderness, the poet's reaction to them is one of indifference; seeing her "comet-like" hair, he squats and yanks the turnip/head up by the root. The poem combines its many tones to reveal a sadness and repressed anger at his daughter's death that is, in its overall effects, astonishing.

The same surreal style is employed in "Telescope with Urn," a poem that addresses the death of another daughter, this one the infant who died in the atomic blast. The first line of the poem refers to the image of galaxies "spread[ing] out like a cloud of sperm": an image that is itself commented upon by an unnamed "observatory guide" who notes its rapid velocity. The image of the galaxies' expansion evokes the expansion of the bomb after impact, all of which contain a strange beauty for the narrator, as the third line suggests: "It is like the idea of the flowers, opening within the idea of the flowers."

From here, the poem takes a more personal turn, as Yasusada recalls his young daughter "squat[ting] over a sky-colored bowl to make water." The poem finishes with this following reference to her death:

> What a big girl!, cried we, tossing you in the general
> direction of the stars.

> Intently, then, in the dream, I folded up the great telescope
> on Mount Horai.

> In the form of this crane, it is small enough for the urn.

Like "Mad Daughter," "Telescope with Urn" uses visual repetition to link its narratives. Galaxies, observatories, sky-colored bowls, and telescopes remind me of the poet's terrified awareness of space. The galaxies are "like a cloud of sperm," which sets me up for the final appearance of the poet's infant daughter who herself gets "tossed up" like ashes or stars. The galaxies open like flowers, which reminds the poet of a monk in the act of flower arranging. Images build one on top of the other, so that the poem begins to "bloom" outward from its initial galactic image. This formal enactment of "flowering" in the poem turns sinister as I realize the final direction the poem takes: the urn containing his daughter's ashes. For me, it's impossible not to see this "flowering" of stars and child as also referencing the physical expansion of the atomic bomb after impact, its eerie and instantaneous explosion, followed by the clouds of ash it leaves. The first image of sperm becomes inextricably linked to the image of nuclear destruction. It's as if Yasusada created a child solely for the purpose of her being destroyed.

I wrote before that my gut desire was to reject these poems once I knew about the hoax. But that's not entirely true, X. My gut desire was to rescue them. And in class, it was easy to rescue these poems, because the students enjoyed discussing them. The poems gave my students difficult topics to consider, and because we could have more engaging conversations about them, I began to see these poems not just as hoaxes but as literature. I even began to wonder in what ways I should consider the hoax itself as part of the work's formal device, a fictional frame that could not be separated from the poems themselves. And in fact, it can't be. Because the reality is that, with racial hoaxes like Yasusada, the context in which the work was produced determines how it must be viewed. Unlike other creative work, the context *is* the work.

When it comes to appropriation, X, most writers, in attempting to represent an identity that is not their own, work to maintain a separation between the author's self and the subject's. In that case, the purpose of the author's imaginative work is to create a representation of an identity that signals her respect, also, for its differences. This kind of writing usually contains within in it some sense of the characters being different from their author: they possess their own intentions, experiences, and private knowledge. When creating a fraudulent identity based on trauma or on a specific racial or ethnic experience, however, no such separation exists. It not only claims the representation of a subject's experience, it claims the subject's very self, suggesting there is something performative about that identity overall. But while identities are shaped through shared cultural performance, X, they are—of course—more than performance. To lose a child to the atomic bomb is not something that is performed, it is an experience that's inflicted.

PSEUDONYMS, CULTURAL FRAUDS, AND
TIME BOMBS

Maybe you're wondering what constitutes writing that claims another's identity, versus writing that hides behind a name. How do you parse the sometimes fine-grained differences between hoaxes? Why are certain fakes culturally appropriative while others aren't? Plenty of writers—myself included—have taken on pseudonymous identities at times, and these identities allow us the freedom either to try out different literary forms and genres, to write in public opposition to popularly held opinions, to publish at times when our true identities would have prevented the work's publication, to sell more books to different audiences, or to keep from offending our families when we write about subjects they don't want associated with themselves. Elena Ferrante, Robert Galbraith, Richard Bachman, Agatha Christie, George Sand, George Eliot, Saki, and O. Henry are a handful of such names. But even as these authors hoodwink readers, they do not attempt to perform any specific or different identity off or on the page. Masking one's name is a form of deception, but it's a socially accepted one that doesn't require that you or I invest the work with biographical authenticity, or a belief in journalistic truth.

There are also writers who create elaborate literary hoaxes, not just to safeguard their careers, but to challenge the publication cultures that would exclude or condescend to them. These include Ossian, purportedly the third-century author of an epic cycle of poems about a Gaelic warrior named Fingal, but who in reality was the eighteenth-century University of Edinburgh professor James Macpherson, who wanted a literary tradition for Scotland that could rival ancient Greece's. Not all long-lived literary hoaxes exploit identity stereotypes, though with

Ossian I might argue that ethnic identity *is* at play, since Macpherson clearly saw his fake as a way to bolster Scottish nationalism. But Macpherson was not trying to write outside the boundaries of his own ethnic identity; rather, he created an idealized version of it for outsiders, one that might carry with it the same weight as more traditionally "important" cultures in the West. Macpherson, in that sense, was not stereotyping another culture, he was trying to write *against* English and Continental stereotypes of Scotland.

The important thing, however, is that—had he not been unmasked—Macpherson would likely have continued. In that, I think the Ossian hoax is different from frauds who *want* to be discovered, frauds like Hudson or Targ, who see their imposture as a joke played on naïve readers. The critic Christopher L. Miller in his book *Imposters: Literary Hoaxes and Cultural Authenticity* calls these fakes "time bombs," as they're meant to go off in readers' faces and unmask the poor judgment of editors. One such bomb was Ern Malley, a poet created in the 1940s by the Australian writers James MacAuley and Harold Stewart, who collaged together quotes from Shakespeare, random phrases from books of quotations, and lines of their own poetry, all to prove how vacuous modern poetry—and modern poetry critics—had become.

Finally, there are racial and cultural hoaxes. One of the most famous ones is JT LeRoy, author of *The Heart Is Deceitful Above All Things*, who turned out not to be a West Virginian, sexually abused male teen and former prostitute with AIDS, but Brooklyn-born Laura Albert, a middle-aged, White female writer for the HBO show *Deadwood*. Albert was uncovered as the hoax's author in the *New York Times* when a reporter received a phone call from her boyfriend revealing Albert's "all-consuming web of deceit." Before that, however, the LeRoy hoax lasted ten years, during which time Albert wrote two novels, a novella, and a film script as LeRoy, and even got her sister-in-law to appear at literary events as LeRoy, costumed in dark sunglasses and a blond wig.

Albert may not conventionally be seen as a transcultural fake because both she and LeRoy are White, but clearly Albert trafficked in communal identities to which she did not belong. An educated, straight, and successful writer living in Brooklyn and San Francisco, Albert pretended to be from rural West Virginia, indigent, the child of a prostitute, and someone whose identity flirted with transgenderism. Worse, Albert tried to pass her persona off as someone dying of AIDS. In court, being sued by the film company that planned to produce her "autobiographical" book, *Sarah*, Albert argued that she'd been sexually abused as a child, and that the trauma from this abuse necessitated her use of a pseudonym and an identity like LeRoy's to write accurately about her experience. Whether or not Albert had actually been abused is up for speculation, but in 2000 when *Sarah* was published, not much was popularly known about transgender people, male prostitutes, or (it seems) West Virginia; it's clear that Albert relied upon these unique elements of LeRoy's identity to be unfamiliar enough that her hoax would be believed.

In that, Albert joins the ranks of a number of writers who've assumed ethnic or racial identities that are not their own. There's *The Education of Little Tree*, by Asa Earl Carter, writing as Forrest Carter, or *Famous All Over Town* by Danny Santiago, who is actually Daniel James. Likely you've never heard of this novel, but *Famous All Over Town* was, in 1983, a very critically acclaimed novel of a young Chicano man growing up poor in East Los Angeles. The author, Daniel James, however, is a White man educated at Andover and Yale who'd struggled to place his stories. With his mentors Gregory Dunne's and Joan Didion's encouragement, James, purportedly out of frustration, changed his last name to Santiago and his debut novel was snapped up. The public reception (and perception) of both Santiago and *Famous All Over Town* was, I think, pretty telling of why the hoax occurred in the first place. When Santiago's editor admitted he'd never met or talked with the author in person, he said, "We figured he was probably in prison and didn't want anyone to know." In the *New York Times*, one reviewer gushed of the novel, "I am totally ignorant of the Chicano urban experience but I have to believe this book is, on that subject, a minor classic."

Cultural hoaxes and frauds are a category of appropriation that lies well outside the norm, and for good reason: they are not meant to be read as imaginative acts of "representative thinking" but taken as real evidence of lived experience. No one questions whether *Light in August* is a novel, thus its portrayals of African Americans are fictional. Faulkner can depict African American culture incorrectly, but the transparency of his project allows and even invites me to make that critique on the basis of his characterization, diction, plot, and style. The transcultural fraud, in comparison, tries to subvert my critique from the artistic representation to the identity itself. It suggests something similar to what my Asian American Poetry students believed: that my aesthetic values are secondary to my notions of cultural authenticity, and that my belief in the fraud signals my own lowering of aesthetic standards in favor of "identity politics."

In that, cultural and racial hoaxes are always built on an idea of inequality, either on the unequal position the appropriated identity holds, or on the self-perception of the writer who has appropriated it. They're also built on the idea that the racialized body is fundamentally unknown or unknowable, a common racist perception of non-White, or non-European, bodies. The poet Kevin Young, in his book *Bunk*, even argues that some of these hoaxes are successful *because* they tap into racist paradigms and metaphors, as he proves with his exploration of the 1835 Moon Hoax, in which the New York paper *The Sun* claimed men had walked on the moon and seen darkly menacing "bat men" on its surface, men with dark and "closely curled hair," their faces like those "of the large orang outing": depictions of otherness that recall the way African Americans, too, were described at the time. If the hoax depends explicitly or implicitly on racial meaning, Young notes, it's because race and hoaxes share something in common. "Race," Young reminds me, "is a fake thing pretending to be real."

I think all of these reasons are why Yasusada is a Japanese victim of Hiroshima, and not a Japanese American formerly interned in an American concentration camp. To evoke an identity that appeals to our national history, Johnson relies upon American historical fascination with U.S. actions in Asia, along with the general American ignorance of Japan. Johnson imagines for the general reader an author who can act as an Orientalist cipher while also gesturing to a familiar critique of our military. At the same time, while his poems may not tap into overt or conventionally racist paradigms you or I might hold about Asians, their exposure as fakes allow a particular kind of reader to indulge the suspicion she might have of the cultural prestige Asians, or other non-White people, possess in the literary marketplace. In that way, Johnson's poems *are* like Targ's and Hudson's: they don't stereotype Asians so much as needle the audience that fetishizes Asian identity.

But with the Yasusada poems, I keep returning to one question:

why did *I* like them? More to the point, if my enjoyment was in any way tied to my belief in the identity of the author, would definitively proving the poems' details are inauthentic cure me of my pleasure? That, X, is the sad genius of these hoaxes. As with our debate around accuracy in *American Dirt*, transcultural hoaxes encourage critics to engage in unwinnable debates that only reveal the paucity of their own racial imaginations. I doubt any American can answer what it means to be "authentically" Japanese without resorting to yet more American stereotypes about Japan. And really, which should carry more weight for me, the poem and its aesthetic attractions, or the knowledge that the poem is a fake? The real issue that troubles me about Yasusada, X, is that, if I was moved by his poems, does that mean I, too, am racist?

If I were looking for ways to discredit Yasusada solely based on Orientalist inaccuracy, there's a lot for me to find. *Doubled Flowering* contains a plethora of conventional symbols for Japan that feel catalogued from a country frozen in the late nineteenth century. Here are geishas and chrysanthemums, sumo wrestlers, references to kabuki, peonies, shakuhachis, the art of calligraphy, *yukatas*, daikon, temples, and monks—all references that begin to feel increasingly like touchstones for an American audience seeking emblems of an exotic and pre-modern Japan. In one unnamed, undated fragment, for instance, the poet lists:

Two daikons

three rice cakes

one (blotted by crease, eds) seaweed packet

4 crane eggs

empress oil   chrysanthemum root   best rice
Beat yourself with a serious air through the labyrinth of the
*   market. Feign to*
ignore the (blotted by crease, eds.) spirit medium of plum-
*   colored lips*

American cologne.

The editors note that "despite the curious interjection, this appears
to be a shopping list" that was "found in one of the notebooks, folded
into an origami bird." Little about this fragment, shopping list or no,
feels believable. Who eats crane eggs? And who buys them based on
a shopping list folded into an origami bird? The exotic cooking items
placed against the reference to some anonymous "American cologne"
feels forced to me, as does the hyperbolic italicized language. In a
few instances in *Doubled Flowering*, Johnson makes references to
American products or perspectives of the Japanese that reveal Yasusada is aware of anti-Asian racism. In these fragments, the Japanese
are suggestively subhuman to Americans, as occurs in this untitled
haiku: "American circus / The Japanese midget wears the body / of a
horse." This awareness for me troubles the Japanese symbols he then
uses in the shopping-list fragment, because they pander to the Western trend of exoticizing the Asian while asserting Occidental dominance. In Yasusada's "shopping list," the list of Japanese goods is
meant to signal their cultural difference from the American cologne,
the goods themselves—both Japanese and American—a symbol for
culture.

But the most damning piece of evidence occurs late in *Doubled Flowering*, in one of its appendices. Apparently in an effort to address the hoax, Kent Johnson and Javier Alvarez wrote an essay that explicitly addressed Johnson's relationship to Yasusada and his own ideas about "the poetry world" as it relates to the avant-garde:

> Indeed, it has been the common assumption for some time in the poetry world that Johnson is the "culprit" of the Yasusada imbroglio, though it is still inadequately explained how a community college Spanish teacher with little poetic talent could have produced work that caused fairly unbridled admiration amongst such a range of well-placed arbiters in the world of poetry.

The barely concealed triumph, anger, and disdain that characterizes this statement unnerves me: am I to understand this project as an attempt by Johnson and Alvarez to frustrate the snobbish world of poetry publishing?

The literary critic Marjorie Perloff has noted that Yasusada's biography and work are riddled with obvious and easily researchable mistakes, including the fact that he claims to have attended a university that had not been founded by the date of his enrollment, that his poetic influences—Spicer and Barthes—either weren't published in Japanese or French at the time of his reading them or weren't known outside their native countries, and that Yasusada's and his wife's very names are used incorrectly by his translators. If I take Perloff's suggestion that these numerous small "mistakes" the authors make regarding the creation of Yasusada's biography are "surely not unintention[al]," that they are, in fact, clues meant to signal that the poems are not legitimate, then can I still see the work as an act of apology?

If Johnson wants to make his poems *both* an imaginative apology *and* a subtle attack on the American poetry scene—an arena from which Johnson imagines himself ejected—then race, culture, and the experience of Hiroshima are being used, and the entire project of empathy is a blind behind which the poet can hide. Yasusada is not just a transcultural hoax but a time bomb, meant to explode in the face of readers who would privilege identity over talent.

THE FANTASY OF FREE IMAGINATIONS

Yasusada was clearly meant to disrupt a publication system that Johnson believed was skewed to favor the writer of color. And sadly, *Doubled Flowering*—if only briefly—succeeded in doing so. Yasusada's work even received a strangely ecstatic reception in the early 2000s after it was determined to be fake: critics rushed to praise what they saw as an exercise of the writer's "free imagination."

But if the argument that experience can be transcended is one that gets subsumed into racist ideology, X, it is also, I think, an argument that cannot always be believed, even by those who support it. When I shared *Doubled Flowering* with my Asian American Poetry class, one student asked if her classmates would equally applaud a Saudi Arabian writing as an American banker who escaped the Twin Towers on 9/11. Much of the class grew visibly upset. My point is that while many of us like the idea of being able to "freely overcome" culture and race and identity, our personal histories and experience of the world make it difficult to accept this. I can tell you until I'm blue in the face that culture or race or memory doesn't matter, X, and that still never stops people from being wounded, even mortally so, by the ways these "constructs" divide us.

But why, again, did I like the poems? Re-reading *Doubled Flowering* now, thirty years after its publication date, I'm reminded of a summer I spent in Japan during my early twenties, in particular the afternoon in which my Japanese host family took me to visit the Hiroshima Peace Memorial. I remember creeping down the hallway of the white stone building, afraid to meet the gaze of the other visitors within. The museum looked both elegant and grotesque: large glass cases displayed artifacts culled from the bombing, along with photographs of victims, remnants of clothing, and copies of official documents. One giant diorama housed an artist's rendering of the bombing's effects upon life-size statues of people. I remember in particular a young girl with her clothes looking seared into her flesh, her limbs bloody and shredded.

At the end of the exhibit was a long, carpeted hall with a few televisions, each programmed to play video recordings of survivors' testaments. The survivors spoke in Japanese, and their statements were translated below in English and French. I sat and watched the videos. Person after person spoke, some with horrible disfigurements, some with a legacy of cancer, some looking physically untouched but anguished. Here was horror and fear, grief, resignation, forgiveness, rage. *I will never forgive America*, one older gentleman said, practically spitting into the camera. *I will never forgive a country that could commit such evil.* The glass windows behind me filled with sun, making it difficult to read the translation. I flinched and squinted. The video had captured a variety of responses to preserve some idea of what Hiroshima meant to those who had experienced it. There was no one reaction, and though I knew each person speaking was a singular

identity, I also understood that the collection of responses was meant
to suggest that all of them together did compose a single identity, the
identity of the Hiroshima survivor, a concept that could and could
not exist. *I forgive them. I despise them. I am suffering. I have made
peace with it. They are evil.* There was nothing coy or elliptical in the
phrases the speakers used. One after the other spoke: man, woman,
man. They blended together, enraged and pained and haunted, a voice
full of ruin. The effect of listening, even for an hour, was agonizing.

Agonizing in a way that the rest of the Peace Museum could
not be. The museum, to be a space anyone can enter, is toned down
from rage and despair to detached elegy. Sadness—not even grief,
which implies a more excruciating loss—is the emotion fostered by
the museum, because sadness can be imaginatively shared. Sadness does not demand. Sadness does not, unlike fury or vengeance,
blame. This is what Johnson's poems achieve for me: his poetry is a
museum of Hiroshima in which the same images recur, posed here
and there like statues in a hallway. Images of space and flowers and
bowls, images of courtship and longing and a distant, occasionally
eerie, sense of absence. Rage doesn't enter Johnson's poems. Nor
does an excess of sorrow. His best poems in fact subvert my feelings
of grief by making them surreal and oddly comical, a subversion I
liked because it didn't implicate *me*. What could be confrontational
was elided or kept on the margins. Johnson's poetry is not an apology to the Japanese. It is an American museum of loss.

EMPATHY AS CULTURAL FANTASY

When a writer pretends to be from an underrepresented identity,
she engages in a high-wire act that knowingly plays on contempo-

rary notions of race and power. By picking and choosing elements of her biography and subject matter, she constructs an identity to appeal to cultural fantasies, part of what formulates Loffreda and Rankine's "racial imaginary." In essence, X, she does something similar to what Katy Perry did in her performance of "Unconditionally": she collapses the person of color with a particular set of values.

Applying Loffreda and Rankine's question about what desire is on display in Yasusada's poems, I can see that Yasusada expresses a particularly American urge to empathize with and to be forgiven by our wartime victims. I can see how much I, too, suffer with this desire. I can see that *Doubled Flowering* purports to overlook race while still depicting certain groups and bodies as traumatic subjects, that the book suggests a need for the reader to believe that an individual is merely a set of arbitrary constructs the White imagination might animate and direct. In the end, what Johnson *hasn't* imagined is an actual Japanese person but an archetype that reifies, rather than subverts, my cultural delusions.

This is why the transcultural or racial hoax is the worst form of cultural appropriation, X. It is not the accidental descent into race as negative metaphor but the deliberate activation of these metaphors. I wrote before that writing is a transgressive act, but the kind of transgression I'm interested in is when the writer, by paying careful attention to the way people unlike her construct their own narratives, subordinates her own authorial entitlement to let other voices through. She does not abbreviate someone else's experience for a private joke, turning legitimate suffering into a grenade she can lob into any public space. The transcultural hoax argues that there is something essential, and ultimately *imitable* about identity. The fact that so many fakes choose the experience of being traumatized—the fake slave narrative, for example, or the fake rape memoir—suggests they see the condition of being a person of color or a woman as itself traumatic. And when critics and readers defend the fake, whether on the basis of imaginative empathy or on the basis of style or on the basis that race itself is a construct, what they defend is the primacy of the White imagination not only to respond to or represent but to *inhabit* other people's narratives. The author's Whiteness comes to authenticate the fake: I praise the audacity of her hoax, I praise the White writer for creating an identity outside her own position, where perhaps I might dismiss the work of a Black poet who writes in the voice of a long-dead Yoruban slave as an expression of identity politics, an extension of skin color rather than talent. If I praise the fake while simultaneously downplaying the work of people of color, I privilege the White writer's imagination with having a cultural power that exceeds that of the non-White one.

But while it is easy to excoriate such frauds as racists, theirs is a racism to which I have learned we are each party. If there is a social use to the hoax, X, it is again to point out the shortcomings of a publication system in which so few voices of color get through. The fake merely responds to our communally held prejudices; she works within the triangulation of money, identity, and representation we ourselves established and protect. The transcultural hoax reminds readers of the terrible potency of our representations. Like it or not, fakes threaten to become an accepted standard of cultural authenticity for underrepresented writers in a system that either cannot or will not distinguish between them.

Sadly, fakes are inevitable when we fetishize difference without working to understand it, or to sensitively represent it in our histories. I think this is how Charles Yu slipped into *Quiet Fire* to begin with and why the book's editor, Juliana Chang, was so embarrassed when I contacted her about the mistake. Though what anthologist, undertaking such a task, wouldn't have desired or even been trained to believe in Yu's existence? In her email to me years ago, Chang wrote that she had learned of the hoax after the book's publication. By that time, it was too late; now she lived with it. The fake in her anthology had become, over time, a real addition.

Currently, the book, published first in 1998, is still in print.

LETTER SIX

Appropriation and Rehabilitation

Dear X:

When I consider why I'm disturbed by my enjoyment of Yasusada, it's partly because I want to have my taste and political sensibilities align. But there have been times in which my politics and my taste have split, usually through my identification with duplicitous or even venal characters, or my interest in whole genres that I sense betrays some more publicly commendable part of me. Why, for example, have I, a feminist, at times thrilled to the most conventional romance novels? Why watch horror movies if I decry violence? For that matter, why am I drawn to Humbert Humbert, why cheer on as well as shudder at Becky Sharpe, and why, *why* do I still keep that Gauguin poster in my pantry?

The tension I feel around Yasusada reminds me that there's a porousness that occurs between writer and reader. The writer shapes a character the reader is invited to see herself in relation to, and in doing so, the reader gives herself up to the text; she relaxes some aspect of her own identity when reading a character. This empathetic elision between text and reader is of course something only the reader can activate, but writers work hard to pierce that veil between self and other that also constitutes writer and reader. This knowledge I have of being manipulated is forgotten in the best literary works, but it's always there in the words writers choose and employ, words whose connotations and denotations can work like magic spells if I'm willing to fall under that particular charm. As a reader, I allow my imagination to become a thing grafted upon by another mind. I take into my memory representations that others have framed for me and adapt them to become another, possibly reverse, image of myself.

And because I'm aware of that as a writer, I understand there's an implicit question of trust built into reading, especially with texts designed to provoke the most painful responses. I'm aware, too, that my hesitation to trust writers might reflect a peculiar point we're at in our cultural history, in which the Internet makes me aware of how texts are produced: who writes them, who publishes them, who purchases them, who is rewarded for them. Writers and the writing world are no longer mysteries. You yourself have taken numerous creative writing classes, as well as met and spoken with dozens of authors on our campus. You can follow all your favorite writers now online, to see what he or she is reading or eating or feuding about any time of the day. You can see their generosity to fellow authors, but also their thoughtless comments, the casual cruelties they engage in. Authors are encouraged by publishers to present their personalities as extensions of their books, thus authors have also become literary commodities, quantifiable if not entirely purchasable, recognizable if not exactly known. Why trust an author, when she behaves so stupidly on social media?

At the same time, however, we've also become more aware of how language in our media is carelessly or ruthlessly deployed. We use metaphor to evoke emotion in poetry, but we also use metaphor to sell "wars" on homelessness, breast cancer, or illegal immigration. Flus become "Chinese viruses"; ethnic groups, "parasites." We use figurative language to obfuscate, to detract, to justify, to pander, as well as to seduce. Why trust words when they have been put to such bad use by politicians and pundits alike?

Maybe it's for these reasons that I begin to want—and need—books to align with my values, either because I do not trust the machinations of my fellow writers, or because I do not trust myself. Our attractions make us vulnerable. And yet, X, even as I write this, I wonder if what I've said is true. Is my imagination *really* grafted upon by another's when I read? Does literature truly lure me to snatch at ideas I would otherwise reject or, because works of literature are tied to their cultural context, do they only reinforce beliefs I have not yet articulated for myself? Does literature actually offer me a space, X, in which I can stand apart from my prejudices?

Likely not, since this would require that I carve out within myself a space utterly untouched by my consciousness. We read through our value systems. But that does not also mean that my value system cannot be *challenged* by my reading, since not all texts espouse the same beliefs and experiences. This is the reason educators include works by diverse authors in the classroom, because they offer readers the possibility of seeing different social realities. It is through the diversity of voices in our reading that, if we are not able to change our convictions entirely, we can reframe what we've been conditioned to believe. As Edward Said noted, cultural and racial groups may be historically intertwined, but these histories separate at crucial moments as well; we cannot argue that people's reactions will always be the same simply "because we're all human," when the term "human" itself has been a categorical definition denied certain people at different points in history.

Likewise, it's not true that I only like texts that reflect the values I hold. As much as my enjoyment of Yasusada's poetry spoke to my need to feel absolved for Hiroshima, I also liked that these poems made me uncomfortable. They gave me and my students difficult ideas to debate; they gave us more, intellectually, to *do*. In our workshop, X, I've tended to treat the study of literature as the acquisition of skills: how to write clear sentences and believable characters, how to craft rich metaphors, or shape your thinking in poetic form and meter. But literature is not a collection of skills. Literature is the expression of conflicting human desires, and reading is the activation of these conflicts, the dynamic engagement with word and idea. Perhaps I might define and identify a work of literature, then, not by whether or not it increases my empathy for others, but whether it unsettles me without a clear resolution. And perhaps I might consider myself a critical reader not because I read Pulitzer Prize–winning novels, but because I'm someone who refuses to be soothed.

Reading Yasusada, I learned I could have multiple desires activated by reading. As a biracial woman, I could challenge the poems. As a writer, I could study them, and as a teacher, I could use them to help students articulate their own ideas about race and identity, history and trauma. All these desires could flow through the same poems, X, at the exact same time. In the end, the value of Yasusada's poetry was less about literary technique than pedagogical engagement.

If I want texts to align with my values and pleasures, then I am asking either for a conventional thriller like *American Dirt*, or a didactic treatise like *The Pilgrim's Progress*. But what I think good readers want, X, is something messier, something that eludes our understanding of "right" and "wrong," "accurate" or "false," "self" and "other," or even "good" or "bad" writing. When texts become literature, it is because they've strayed outside our ideas of specific lanes; their flaws and deckle edges become meaningful inroads to understanding the larger ideas the texts themselves suggest, which is why I can teach a novel like *Dracula*—that soapy, Gothic potboiler—to serious effect in seminars. Bad writing can serve a useful purpose to me as teacher, X, something I've come to consider an important literary value.

Throughout these letters I've argued against thinking of reading as a fundamentally empathetic or moral endeavor. And yet reading does hold social value; I believe literature should make readers more self-conscious and flexible, self-critical, and also open-minded. Good reading should make me resistant to demagoguery. In that sense, if I don't believe reading is a moral endeavor, I do believe it is a critical skill with moral effects, and that these effects become more pronounced the more carefully I attend to my reading. So perhaps we should take reading and writing with some moral seriousness: how can literature make us see more complexity, more nuance, more differentiation in humans, not less?

But if I have argued against using empathy as a critical tool, I do believe it's crucial to sustaining literary communities. Because what, exactly, is the value of disdain? How much is my criticism worth, X, if I believe it should only or finally humiliate the author? If my only response to work that imaginatively fails is to say that the writer is racist or sexist or ableist, that is an attempt to end a more complicated discussion about appropriation by slapping a label on a person that confuses her with the text she has produced. Labeling her puts her outside the scope and pressure of my forgiveness; it allows me to indict her without offering myself any opportunity to forgive her.

Forgiveness, of course, is not required of any community or readership. It is and should not be automatically granted and, in some cases, it may not be possibly practiced. But it should, I think, remain a communal goal. A long literary career means that you will work with dozens of writers and editors and publishers, some of whom will behave monstrously, most of whom will be kind, generous, and thoughtful. Your creative life will be entwined with people who have demonstrated less than exemplary behavior; you, too, will give and take offense, perhaps even publishing work you will come to wish had never seen the light of day. I myself have committed a number of appropriative offenses over the course of my life. When I was nineteen and in my first workshop, I wrote a poem about blindness in which I used blind people as a metaphor for—wait for it—spiritual blindness, and was rightly excoriated by a classmate who worked at an institute for the blind. I recently received a deservedly scolding email from a poet who'd read an homage I'd written of his work that hadn't given him explicit attribution. And, more to the point of these letters, I wrote a hybrid memoir entitled *Intimate*, which details the life of the photographer Edward Sheriff Curtis and also the life of one of his American Indian guides, a man named Alexander Upshaw. I made both men characters in my book to explore the ways that White modernity has worked to erase both Native and mixed-race people from the American historical record.

In all honesty, I didn't want to write about Alexander Upshaw. I knew what I was risking, and I knew what my voice would be taking away, and from whom, even as I believed Upshaw's story was central to the book. The more I wrote about Curtis, and the way my family loved his photographs, the more clearly I saw how I'd included no Native voices in my book to critique Curtis's vision and my family's response. Upshaw was, I realized, not an incidental figure but a crucial one to reframing how I saw Curtis's photographs of American Indians. I had no desire to write about Upshaw out of creative curiosity; instead, I had a great desire to write about Upshaw as a figure of critical resistance.

The book is obviously an example of subject appropriation, but is it also a racist cultural appropriation? I researched, I studied, I shared my work with a host of different readers and editors, I researched more, and I listened. Some critics rejected the work as an act of cultural appropriation, while others applauded it as a success. Obviously, I'd like to believe the latter critics, but the former ones might actually be right. In the end, I'm not the one who gets to decide, X. That's the role of critics and readers. That's the role of time. I understand every possible response to *Intimate*. And I respect the communities I wrote about enough to accept their criticism.

If you truly believe that a more representative and open literary community allows for more creative freedom for everyone, then you have to imagine ways that a community can include and, yes, rehabilitate as many voices and people as possible, even as it struggles to represent and include as many new voices as it can. Because the fact is, at some point or other, each of us will be on the receiving end of criticism, and each of us needs the painful opportunity to change.

REHABILITATION AND RECUPERATION

The more I think about it, however, the more I think that perhaps "rehabilitation" isn't the word I want to use with regard to art that imaginatively fails. Perhaps the word I really mean for such work is "recuperation." I was thinking this just the other day, during a conversation with a professor friend who'd admitted, sheepishly, that he was afraid to teach John Berryman to his graduate students. "I can't do it," he admitted, referring to the minstrel-show language Berryman employs in certain poems from *Dream Songs*. "I think it's too dangerous."

"Dangerous" is a telling word, because it suggests that he *would* teach the poems if he felt his students, keen perhaps to sniff out every ethical offense, wouldn't hassle him. But with Berryman, I should hope the students *would* be offended. They'd be right to point out Berryman's use of minstrel dialect that he uses to structure some of his sonnets. But in pointing out Berryman's occasional and cartoonish dialect, they would also have to note his use of absurdly medieval rhetoric, too, his tortured syntax, his use of baby talk and song snippets and random stress marks over syllables, his neologisms. They would have to point out that Henry, Berryman's alter ego, is a conglomeration of references and languages, of Id-like impulses and superego control mechanisms all fighting to represent, and master, Henry. Henry and Berryman are never trying to perform any one specific idea of Black identity. They are instead performing the barely suppressed rages, depressions, desires, racism, and urges that compose the middle-class White man trying, desperately, not to follow in his father's footsteps and commit suicide. The specter of the minstrel is not the Black man, it is White Henry.

Perhaps that is not enough to convince you that Berryman is worth reading in our class. The tropes of the minstrel performance are and can only be racist, you tell me: that is its place in history, and any art that appropriates its tropes can never be rescued.

It's true that the minstrel show is racist, X. But to say that the minstrel show is racist is also the least interesting critical thing you can say about the minstrel show. I take it as a given that certain performances and types of speech from certain periods of time are racist—even if that language and those performances were not generally conceived to be racist at the time. The critical questions about race and performance we apply to literature must be more expansive than that, if we are to have any relationship to the literature of the past. So after we acknowledge that the literature we study together is racist, what does rethinking the presence of this language, this dialogue, this character, this particular performance of race mean to how we perceive and construct our imagination of racial identity now, both for the White reader, and for the person of color?

For me, though I've struggled with Berryman's minstrel language, I've also learned a great deal through teaching his *Dream Songs* about how to construct a multiply voiced self on the page. In studying Berryman, I've learned how to collage together language in ways that are both playful and disruptive to my idea of an "autobiographical" poem. I also understood that I did not have to duplicate his values exactly or even in part to gain these effects, even as I took the lessons about identity that he offered seriously: each of us is a performance of self that corresponds, roughly, to the theories of self that hold sway at the time.

Of course, I understand that this repositions the conversation, again, around Whiteness, reifying the argument that people of color are present in literature to bolster the White imagination. But I also understand that Whiteness is a slippery thing to identify, and often can only be seen in its paranoid re-creations of raced selves. I also recognize that teaching Berryman requires a particular trust that students like you must have in me as a teacher: am I a teacher who presents poems merely to shock you into uncomfortable responses? Or am I a teacher who's thoughtfully considered the poems she brings to class, and chooses work not only because it's "canonical" but because it helps facilitate larger conversations you might have around poetry? If I teach Berryman just because other people have taught him, that's a fairly unexamined pedagogy. How I present Berryman in class demands that I contextualize and question *all* the ways I might read him, and how you might then respond to my teaching. Finally, I don't think that Berryman can be taught in a vacuum. Berryman's voice becomes particularly important when placed against other writers working at the time, not just Robert Lowell and Sylvia Plath and Anne Sexton, but Amiri Baraka, Ralph Ellison, and Toni Cade Bambara. If Berryman were the only voice allowed in the room, I, too, would cease to teach Berryman.

Perhaps, X, you think the lessons Berryman can teach us—that identity is only a performance—will only please White audiences best, since this lesson satisfies something White people experience but people of color do not, as Whiteness can put on and take off masks while the mask remains firmly glued to the face of the person of color. Surprisingly, this is one more thing I think Berryman's minstrelsy may be, if not consciously then accidentally, reminding us of. If I go beyond the limitations built into Berryman's poem to be able to reach that conclusion about identity as it exists off the page, isn't teaching Berryman worth it to help students learn how to articulate that?

Here's a question to ask: was Berryman's use of minstrel dialect meant to be only and finally racist? Was *The Confessions of Nat Turner*? Meredith's "Effort at Speech"? I hope you can understand the difference between deliberately activated racist speech and speech that engages thoughtlessly in racism; it's like the distinction between pornography and a story that includes a badly written passage about sex. Perhaps you do not care to make that distinction, X, but for me that distinction has been crucial, because even if it cannot rescue certain texts, it has allowed me greater access to literary devices from which I, as a writer, have learned. Granted, reading Berryman or Styron or Meredith was not painful for me as it has been painful for others, but there have been many other texts that *have* been painful for me to study. I've learned to separate myself critically from what I read, which is one more reason I think we should remind ourselves that empathy is not the only and ultimate value of reading, because if the writer does not have access to all that I know and feel and believe, I do not have to inhabit all that *she* knows, values, and believes.

What strikes me, X, as I write this, is that when I worry that my attraction to certain authors makes me a racist, perhaps I am making a simplistic connection between myself and these authors. My connection is analogous to the ways in which we conjoin people with the ideas they express, saying, in effect, that when one expresses a racist belief, that person herself is a racist. But the strange reality of people is that they can express both racist and anti-racist ideas, even in the same conversation; people often drift between positions we might assume would be impossible for a single person to hold. This is why Ibram X. Kendi argues that we need to distinguish between the person and the idea, to recognize that people can hold contradictory beliefs about race while also requiring people to reevaluate the logic that underpins their racist thinking. Literary texts, too, move between racist and anti-racist sentiments, and trying to classify a text or author solely as "racist" or "not racist" forces us to make reductive determinations about textual meaning, authorship, and history that ultimately is a diminishment of both the text and our critical reading practice.

Which gets to another point about the problematic ways we've elevated empathy as a fundamental reading value in our culture, treating writing as if it were not just an act of language but of soul-making: at some point, I'm going to read texts that either include ideas that do not move me, that do not speak to me, that do not reflect or even suggest my experience in the world, and that might profoundly offend me on almost every level that matters. I do not have to learn any valid literary technique or way of living from these texts, but I do have to learn how to stand up against them. I have to learn how to confront language that distresses me and not feel my world crumble but solidify in response to it. In many ways, I was able to become a writer *because* my opinions were in opposition to the books I'd read, and because my own reality as a biracial woman was not always reflected—or reflected positively—in the literature I studied. Being able to identify that a text contains more than one possibility of reading and critique gave me a greater command over my own imagination. Over the years, I have learned to pick apart arguments that offend me so as to strengthen my own technique and beliefs in response to them. This is what literature majors are trained to do.

Of course, if my professor friend considered all these issues and still decided that the value of teaching Berryman was vastly outweighed by his deployment of a racist vaudeville performance, that's a valid choice. But that choice does not automatically render another teacher's choice to continue teaching Berryman as racist. These options are not mutually exclusive, X; they exist along a continuum of questions you and I can have about texts whose authors, and whose subject matters, present ethical problems around reading.

THE CULTURAL IMPORTANCE OF LITERARY FAILURE

If texts are tied to their historical context and meaning, this of course limits their claims to being "objective" portraits and representations of their characters' racial identities, but it also suggests a means of recuperation and reevaluation for writers who, in our current political climate, fail. Brian Morton, a novelist and professor, published a recent *New York Times* editorial entitled "Virginia Woolf? Snob! Richard Wright? Sexist! Dostoyevsky? Anti-Semite!" that I think makes an elegant case for this. Morton argues that we might approach reading the work of dead writers we don't politically agree with as a kind of time machine that lets us walk into the writer's world, while keeping the writer outside of our own. This isn't to say that I abandon my values when reading, but that I ask myself to treat the attitudes, the beliefs, and the philosophies of these writers as cultural artifacts. They are the flotsam and jetsam of people now foreign to me, whose beliefs I know from the beginning of my journey do not and will not match up with my own. By doing this, Morton says, we are not only prepared to see the differences in our beliefs, we might even be able to parse out some of the complexities these writers' moral failings offer us as readers. There is real value in being able to see how one writer's anti-Semitism differed from the anti-Semitism of the time, for example. It also gives me a world view that is more nuanced because I see in myself the same potential moral fallibility: If a writer as smart as Wharton got race wrong, what am I getting wrong now?

I think a writer like William Faulkner offers up a fascinating case study for Morton's argument. With regards to writing about African Americans, Faulkner's work leaps back and forth, in large part because Faulkner's own opinions about race changed dramatically over his life. Letters to his father while Faulkner was a student at Yale, for example, pronounce smugly that Blacks up North "are not as happy or contented as ours are," and that "all this freedom does is to make them more miserable because they are not white." His early novels and essays alternately portrayed miscegenation as a terrible stain to be avoided, and also as the future hope for a racially unified South. Faulkner's very first Yoknapatawpha novel, *Flags in the Dust*, portrays the African American Strother family according to Southern stereotypes of the day: a criminal father, a lying son, a promiscuous mother who sleeps with a White man to produce a mixed-race child. Compounding this depiction of the Strothers is Faulkner's extended metaphor of one worker he describes like a mule, "with its trace-galled flanks and flopping, lifeless ears, and its half-closed eyes drowsing venomously behind pale lids, apparently asleep with its own motion . . . [u]gly, untiring, and perverse."

Only a few years later, however, Faulkner publishes *The Sound and the Fury*, with its self-sacrificing character Dilsey Gibson, the Black servant and maternal figure for the Compson children, a woman who's arguably the novel's beating heart. Dilsey is an evolutionary leap forward for Faulkner, though if you're looking for active resistance to White racism in the novel you certainly won't find an example of that in Dilsey, whose greatest hope for racial liberation comes via her Christian belief in the afterlife. Faulkner argues that Dilsey's redemption, her freedom from the painful legacy of slavery, will come only in death, an argument that may strike us now as too conservative, even as Faulkner also showed more compassion and insight into Dilsey's experience than most other White Southern writers could demonstrate at the time.

Faulkner depicted Black characters as villains and as heroes, he argued for educational integration, and he also admitted that, if African Americans rioted in his hometown, he might be forced to shoot them. In 1931, he published the staunchly anti-lynch-law story "Dry September"; it was the same year he sent a letter to the Memphis *Commercial-Appeal* that virtually defended lynching, stating "[T]here is one curious thing about mobs. Like our juries, they have a way of being right."

You can see how Faulkner struggled with racist thinking, in ways that might be both profoundly familiar and unfamiliar to you. If you apply Morton's time-machine strategy to reconsidering Faulkner and race, it might be useful for you now to consider the other visual and literary texts produced about African Americans during the most prolific period of Faulkner's life. So here's a quick list: *Birth of a Nation* was produced in 1915, and the African American filmmaker Oscar Michaux's critical response to it, *Within Our Gates*, appeared in 1920. *Show Boat*, with its infamous and sympathetic miscegenation subplot, came to theaters in 1927, while the wildly popular, Pulitzer Prize–winning play, *Ol' Man Adam an' His Chillun*, written by White playwrights Roark Bradford and Marc Connelly, hit Broadway in 1928. If you don't know it, *Ol' Man Adam an' His Chillun* was a comic rendition of the Old Testament rewritten in Black dialect. Its point, if you can't tell by the title, was to poke fun at African Americans.

Thus the period in which Faulkner wrote his Yoknapatawpha novels was defined by its fears of and fascination with miscegenation, its terror of race riots, its growing awareness of lynching in the

South, and its racist appropriation of Black popular culture. Place Faulkner in this context, and you might gain a more nuanced appreciation for his ideas about the South and African Americans; you can certainly start to see where his ideas about race were both imitative *and* innovative. Looking at Faulkner this way helps me to see the cultural web of connections in which both his—and later, my—ideas of racial tolerance have been spun.

I experienced something like Morton's time machine while reading "Indian Camp." At first, reading through my contemporary lens and values, I could only see it as a failure. Once I situated myself within Hemingway's time frame, and once I knew of other texts like Higginson's poem and Edward Curtis's photos, however, I could tease out the slippages in Hemingway's writing that, while never fundamentally changing the story, complicated my first reading of it. I could see where Hemingway swallowed the Vanishing Race trope whole, and I could also see where he wanted us to be distrustful of Nick's father. It's not a story that writing students should study as a model, but I think it is a story that teaches us much about American literature.

Because while "Indian Camp" is a racist depiction of Native identity, it's also an example of how pervasive the Vanishing Race trope once was. Once you see that, you can see how often we *still* replicate that trope in our films, our literature, and our art. Certainly, the Native characters in "Indian Camp" don't teach us anything about being indigenous, but they do teach us a lot about how Whiteness in literature has constructed itself in reaction to its ideas of indigeneity.

I teach Asian American literature, X, and one story I regularly bring to class is Jack London's "The Unparalleled Invasion." It's a work of speculative fiction that London published in 1910 in *McClure's*, and it's a response to the early-twentieth-century American anxiety about a growing Chinese workforce on U.S. shores. In London's story, the Chinese are depicted as automatons, psychologically satisfied only by continual labor, and terrifyingly fertile. Their burgeoning population threatens the livelihood of White workers across the world, as well as Western art and culture itself, thus America and Europe release a plague into China that wipes out the bulk of its population. All fleeing survivors are summarily slaughtered by the Western armies that have gathered along the Chinese border, to prevent any individuals from escaping and breeding. China falls, to be repopulated by Europeans and Americans, who have together rescued the world from the Chinese invasion.

The story, if you can't tell, is trash. But the story also has significant cultural value. Students, perhaps taught *The Call of the Wild* or "To Build a Fire" in middle school, are stunned to see a well-regarded author like London deploying such racist images, and stunned further to learn that his sentiments were common in early-twentieth-century literature and journalism. They may also be surprised by how contemporary London's racism sounds in a pandemic–afflicted political landscape. London's story gives my students a context for how to read later writing by Asian American writers around labor, immigration, and even speculative fiction itself.

Perhaps it's obvious to you that all texts have both literary and cultural value, and that "value" itself is just as dependent on historical meaning and intertextual connection as much as on aesthetic interest, but not all readers believe this. Readers in the '90s didn't always believe this either, when critics struggled over Faulkner's depictions of African Americans, or in the '60s, when people hotly debated the merits of Styron's novel in magazines like *Vanity Fair*. My argument around context and cultural studies gets made every thirty years or so, as we readjust our critical understanding of race and representation, and with it our ideas of canonicity and inclusion. We will never have perfect depictions of race, or perfect models for how to imagine race, because we have imperfect beliefs about race. So instead of discarding all texts that could neither anticipate nor correspond with our contemporary sensibilities, perhaps we might ask what, if anything, we might want to recuperate from them, so that these works can continue to educate us as readers of history, if not as models of humanistic merit.

Finally, lest you think I'm decrying as too sensitive or anti-intellectual the students who would take Berryman to task, I'm grateful for the outrage. How else will teachers like me be encouraged to revise what we've been taught, implicitly, to think? How else will writers like you innovate and expand your representational and publication practices without some critical pressure? If I believe that to read the past, and to read widely in the past, is not to doom students to a lifetime of therapy, why should a healthy suspicion of canonical texts lead only to anti-intellectualism?

Here are some questions you might ask yourself with regard to reading appropriative works: Do you require that authors write socially approved depictions of race, or will you also accept realistic reactions people have about race, which means that at some level there is a value in reading work that expresses racist sentiments? If appropriation can be more than the performance of racial stereotypes and meanings, can you teach yourself to be tolerant of it as a literary practice, while also challenging how some have used appropriation to highlight the socially constructed aspects of racial identity in ways that only benefit the White imagination? In what ways can appropriation allow each of us to delve more honestly into the complexities that compose racial difference? And what does honesty mean when readers so casually apply that term to writing that offends?

HONESTY AND RACIAL SELF-REFLECTION

Here's a poem about race once championed as just such an honest exploration of Whiteness. It was published by Tony Hoagland in 2003, and it's called "The Change."

> The season turned like the page of a glossy fashion magazine.
> In the park the daffodils came up
> and in the parking lot, the new car models were on parade.
>
> Sometimes I think that nothing really changes—
>
> The young girls show the latest crop of tummies,
>   and the new president proves that he's a dummy.
>
> But remember the tennis match we watched that year?
> Right before our eyes
>
> some tough little European blonde
> pitted against that big black girl from Alabama,
> cornrowed hair and Zulu bangles on her arms,
> some outrageous name like Vondella Aphrodite—
>
> We were just walking past the lounge
>   and got sucked in by the screen above the bar,
> and pretty soon

we started to care about who won,

putting ourselves into each whacked return
as the volleys went back and forth and back
like some contest between
the old world and the new,

and you loved her complicated hair
and her to-hell-with-everybody stare,
and I,
            I couldn't help wanting
the white girl to come out on top,
because she was one of my kind, my tribe,
with her pale eyes and thin lips

and because the black girl was so big
and so black,
                    so unintimidated,

hitting   the   ball   like   she   was   driving   the   Emancipation
      Proclamation
down Abraham Lincoln's throat,
like she wasn't asking anyone's permission.

There are moments when history
passes you so close
            you can smell its breath,
you can reach your hand out
                    and touch it on its flank,

and I don't watch all that much *Masterpiece Theatre*,
but I could feel the end of an era there

in front of those bleachers full of people
in their Sunday tennis-watching clothes

as that black girl wore down her opponent
then kicked her ass good
then thumped her once more for good measure

and stood up on the red clay court
holding her racket over her head like a guitar.

And the little pink judge
                    had to climb up on a box
to put the ribbon on her neck,
still managing to smile into the camera flash,
even though everything was changing

and in fact, everything had already changed—

Poof, remember? It was the twentieth century almost gone,
we were there,

and when we went to put it back where it belonged,
it was past us
and we were changed.

You might remember that I taught this poem in our class last spring, because you and the other students were curious about examples of White writers who explored their own racial identity. The poem isn't an example of cultural appropriation in its strictest sense, as Hoagland never attempts to imagine the interior life of "Vondella Aphrodite," but it feels appropriative to readers because it deploys racist imagery in order to give its White narrator a veneer of authentic self-examination. Essentially, Hoagland uses a caricature of Serena Williams to make the White character's admission of his own racism more appealing.

Hoagland wasn't a poet you or the other students knew, though he'd been popular in the late '90s and early aughts, before "The Change" sparked a fraught hallway conversation between Hoagland and Claudia Rankine, both colleagues at the University of Houston at the time, which then turned into a national confrontation when Hoagland brusquely dismissed Rankine's questions about Hoagland's portrayal of Serena Williams in an open letter she published on the internet. "The Change" led to a nationwide call for poets and writers to articulate their ideas about Whiteness, which formed the basis of the anthology *The Racial Imaginary*, as well as a national conference for writers of color, and also helped inspire *Citizen*, Rankine's hybrid text exploring race, microaggressions, and the continued artistic misrepresentation and erasure of African Americans.

The fact you hadn't heard of Hoagland was, perhaps, ironic evidence in support of Hoagland's thesis: a change is coming, and it would overtake people like Hoagland. I clearly remember the debate circling Hoagland's poem when it first appeared, and the ways many writers—White and non-White—tried to defend the poem on the basis of its honesty. "Honesty," however, was the last word that came to my mind after reading it again. In fact, the poem is not at all honest in its exploration of race, nor in its treatment of the speaker's own racism. The speaker's racist imagery is simply dropped on the page. The poem refuses to interrogate this imagery either actively or contextually, as Patricia Smith's "Skinhead" does by tying Skinhead's racism to his understanding of class and gender, and the failed promises of American history. Rather than taking a prominent cultural figure and diminishing her, as Hoagland does, Smith's poem takes a reviled person and uses what has diminished him as a source of compassionate connection. Hoagland, in contrast, seems to have no sense of what constrains him. Hoagland's speaker's class and gender are implied but unexamined except through physical depictions of the speaker's body, with its "thin lips" and "pale" features. In that, his speaker's understanding of racial difference is solely physical, even ethnological, which the speaker acknowledges when he calls the White eastern European female tennis player one "of [his] tribe."

A poem engaged in a more self-critical examination of race might here stop to interrogate that word "tribe," and the speaker's belief that race trumps shared citizenship, leading to an elucidation of what the speaker understands to be his own national and racial identity. Instead, you can see that the poem leaves the phrase dangling, much as it tosses out a whole parade of suggestive insults, including the Black tennis player's name, and the speaker's exaggerated sense of her physical size and animal characteristics. Even history itself is changed from an abstract concept into a real, physical body that recalls that of the Black tennis player, something with a "flank" one can "reach . . . out and touch."

None of these images, however closely they might approximate or render the speaker's previously unexpressed feelings about African Americans, is treated as more than a joke in the poem. As you and your classmates noted, Hoagland's sentiments are casually

expressed, and in that, unearned. "The Change" traffics in stereotypes, but does nothing to allow the reader a lens through which
to critique those stereotypes with the speaker, without dismissing
the speaker himself, something the poem resists, as the speaker's
use of the "we" pronoun continually entices the reader to identify
with him. "The Change" is a provocation masquerading as an intimate examination of one's racism, much in the way the insult about
a friend's tired appearance gets downplayed when I insist it's merely
an "honest" assessment of her looks.

Discussing this poem with you so many—and also so few—years
after its publication was to experience for myself the powerful shift
that has occurred in our culture. Entering the classroom, I'd armed
myself to show you how Hoagland's poem failed; during the conversation, however, I felt I needed to protect it, so effectively did you all
eviscerate both it and Hoagland. I found myself bemused, thinking
back to the high-flown debates about "The Change" I'd seen played
out between writers in literary journals, realizing now there would
be no more debate: our ideas had evolved enough that "The Change"
was lost to readers like you and me, tossed into the same critical dust
bin as "Indian Camp" or "The Unparalleled Invasion." It made me a
little giddy. For a moment, my memories of hissed hallway conversations overheard between White colleagues bemoaning how "we'll
never hire a good one of *those* people" disappeared, taking with it the
fear drilled into me as a student that writing about my identity would
be viewed as anti-intellectual or sentimentally self-serving. Gone the
self-hatred absorbed from years of subtle snubbing in workshops and
at conferences. All of it, for a second, blissfully melted away. The needle had moved. We had moved it.

And then the next week, signs began appearing around campus. IT'S OK TO BE WHITE, these signs read in big, bold, Arial font, taped to metal poles around the university, and I thought again about Hoagland's poem, and I thought, too, about the deep and painful ambivalence about Whiteness in twentieth-century America that Hoagland likely felt and meant to have written in that poem, meant to have written but failed to write, and died before he ever could write it. And I felt something then that I couldn't name: not rage and not despair either, but a kind of depthless, vibrating exhaustion. What had changed, really? And what has not changed? How is it we are continually moving and yet staying in place, both at the same time?

If I were honest with you, X, I'd admit I'm tired of thinking about race. I'm tired of quietly bracing myself during interactions with strangers who may or may not be suddenly curious about "where I'm from." And I'm tired of worrying that I'm offending strangers in turn, of negotiating the tricky obstacle course that allows me to respect racial difference without assigning racial meaning to it. I'm tired of the daily paradox that racial knowledge presents me with, which is that we can never escape racial meaning and its implied hierarchies of power, even as I know that constantly attending to such difference and its meaning in the world is driving me insane.

So long as I imagine people first by their racial meaning in society, I cease to see some crucial part of them. We each become cogs in an ever-grinding machinery, and in that, we lose individuation. If I apply this knowledge to my creative work, I risk producing art that makes my characters vapid, their actions predetermined on the page because their social meanings are allegorical. How can I portray anyone truthfully or respectfully if I only see her as a reflection of a system? And yet, how can I portray her at all if I ignore the system in which she's been forged?

I think the paradox of literary appropriation replicates the paradox of racial awareness in the world, which is that we each must acknowledge how our imaginations are both contained within and are kept independent from larger systems of power. We may not be free of our histories, our families, our communities, our appearance, and our health, we may not even be released from all our desires, but we are also not automatons unable to respond to the systems in which we function. Language shapes us, but as writers, we shape language in turn. If you don't believe you're capable of that, X, you will remain at the mercy of other people's representations, ensnared in the tropes, narratives, and metaphors they imagine for you.

Appropriation, also, does not only work in one direction. Even a quick look around at the things I eat, wear, read, watch, and listen to reveals how interconnected we've become in our performances of self. The commodification of art and aesthetics means that you and I are encouraged to appropriate, and that so long as we participate in a market-driven system, our ability to preserve one another's art forms and objects as culturally distinct will fail. That said, I do not want to suggest that we center money in our discussion of the arts, since that treats literature primarily as capital. By suggesting that the true power of creative art is about generating such capital, we jealously enforce the rules about who makes, how they make, and what they make.

Most of my life I've had to wrest my ideas of creative success away from my desires for financial gain. As you can imagine, this is pretty easy for a poet to do. But by separating out my art from its social and economic meaning, I've also come to see the poem as a space that, while public in its reception, is not necessarily one that has to duplicate the values of the public. I mean, X, that I can use my art to put different ideas and values in contention with one another. Literature offers me the space for dissent, not just thoughtless replication, and it is this complexity that comprises literature's most transgressive force, allowing us to see our differences treated with respect because they are acknowledged to exist.

If you and I treat appropriation as a creative act that holds *only certain individuals* captive inside social meanings, rather than understand it as a practice that engages each of us daily, I think we deny ourselves full intellectual, commercial, and artistic agency; we treat ourselves, or others, merely as victims of the systems in which we live. But appropriation is not only or finally a way to reify conventional social inequalities and racist power structures: we may find that appropriation helps us to critique the very systems that fail to represent us. Which leads me to my final questions, X: If, as I argued before, reading literature serves a moral purpose, and if appropriation is so entwined in our literary practice, does appropriation then offer readers a particular redemptive purpose? We know what appropriation ethically risks, but what might it also ethically reward?

THE ETHICS OF APPROPRIATING CULTURES

With these questions in mind, there's one last story I want to share with you. It's Percival Everett's "Appropriation of Cultures," from his 2004 volume of short stories, *Damned If I Do*. "Appropriation of Cultures" is a provocative examination of the knot that binds Black and White Southern culture, in particular the ways in which this tie provides the story's young, African American narrator, Daniel Barkley, a way to neutralize certain symbols of White racism.

The story opens with a description of Daniel that includes

almost everything he owns and has inherited. The paragraph includes everything the general reader should know about Daniel; everything, that is, except for his racial identity.

> Daniel Barkley had money left to him by his mother. He had a house that had been left to him by his mother. He had a degree in American Studies from Brown University which he had in some way earned but had not yet earned anything for him. He played a nineteen-forty Martin guitar with a Barkus-Berry pickup and drove a nineteen-seventy-six Jensen Interceptor which he had purchased after his mother's sister had died and left him her money, she having had no children of her own. Daniel Barkley didn't work and didn't pretend to need to, spending most of his time reading. Some nights he went to a joint near the campus of the University of South Carolina and played jazz with some old guys who all worked very hard during the day, but didn't hold Daniel's condition against him.

Everett's statement that the "old guys . . . didn't hold Daniel's condition against him" is a subtle reference to Daniel's class and education, but a reader could be forgiven for thinking it might refer to Daniel's racial difference. In fact, these older men aren't racially identified either, except implicitly through the jazz they play and explicitly through the interactions they have with a group of "white boys from a fraternity" who come to the club and demand they play "Dixieland."

The White boys are immediately racially identified, but it takes a minute to place Daniel, who eyes the boys and, in part to protect the older musicians, in part to shame the fraternity boys, begins to play

"Dixieland" and, to both his and the reader's surprise, take ownership of the song.

> He used the slide to squeeze out the melody of the song he had
> grown up hating, the song the whites had always pulled out to
> remind themselves and those other people just what they were.
> Daniel sang the song. He sang it slowly. He sang it, feeling the
> lyrics, deciding the lyrics were his, deciding the song was his . . .
> He sang the song and listened to the silence around him. He
> resisted the urge to let satire ring through his voice. He meant
> what he sang. *Look away, look away, look away, Dixieland.*

It is at this moment that I clearly know Daniel is African American,
and yet Everett's prose stays slippery with this fact. The White fraternity boys request the song to humiliate the musicians, but Everett's
syntax doesn't quite let them do this. The song, Daniel notes, is "to
remind themselves and *those other people* (emphasis mine) just what
they were." The song is and is not meant for Daniel, one of "those
other people" who are, Everett implies, African American, and yet
Everett's syntax also disassociates Daniel psychologically from the
song's intended audience. This small detail is an act of resistance
on Daniel's part, and possibly helps him make the decision to claim
the song as his own. Daniel "decid[es] the lyrics [are] his," and so he
sings the song without irony.

And yet Daniel recognizes that his playing of the song *is*, in fact,
historically ironic. He recognizes that "as he played [the song], it
came straight from his heart, as he was claiming southern soil, or at
least recognizing his blood in it. His was the land of cotton and hell
no, it was not forgotten." When Daniel returns home that night, he

dreams of stopping Civil War general George E. Pickett's soldiers on Emmitsburg Road and telling them, "Give me back my flag."

Daniel imaginatively appropriates "Dixieland" and the Confederate flag, much as he later appropriates an actual Confederate flag on the back of a pickup truck he buys from a working-class White couple. For Daniel, Southern history and culture is not automatically White, though it has certainly been appropriated by Whites as a symbol of their authority, and purported supremacy. But Daniel recognizes that the violence of White power could not exist without the existence and resistance of African Americans; in that, "Dixieland" and the Confederate flag are his, too, as shocking a concept as that is initially to Daniel's Black female friend, Sarah, and even to the White couple, Travis and Barb, who sell Daniel their truck. Barb in particular keeps asking Daniel if he really wants to keep the Confederate flag sticker on the back windshield.

> Barb sighed and asked as if the question was burning right through her. "Why do you want that flag on the truck?"
>
> "Why shouldn't I want it?" Daniel asked.
>
> Barb didn't know what to say. She studied her feet for a second, then regarded [Daniel's] house again. "I mean, you live in a nice house and drive that sports car. What do you need a truck like that for?"
>
> "You don't want the money?"
>
> "Yes, we want the money," Travis said, trying to silence Barb with a look.

Here, Barb deflects the awkward conversation Daniel has invited about racism by noting Daniel's comfortable economic position, trying to pretend it's his wealth, not his race, that should make the truck undesirable. In this, Barb's comment is not unlike Everett's opening paragraph, which positions Daniel among objects and an education that he possesses but that also possess him in our imaginations of his racial identity. He is wealthy, expensively educated, musically gifted, and steeped in American Studies. Daniel has inherited and also purchased a class status that I might stereotypically associate with Whiteness, and it allows him to see the way in which class interacts visibly and invisibly—but always powerfully—with race.

Of course, Daniel is not innocent in his purchasing power. He plays blues and jazz with older, working-class musicians who don't see Daniel as like them because Daniel doesn't have to work. The title of the story is "Appropriation of Cultures," plural, and if Daniel uses his money to appropriate White symbols of power, I think a critic like Baraka could also argue that Daniel appropriates Black working-class culture too. But if Daniel exists at a nexus between various class and racial cultures, so too, Everett's story suggests, do we all. Sarah, Daniel's Black friend, asks Daniel if she should paint her nails "with red, white and blue stripes." Barb and Travis, White and poor, have appropriated a historical Civil War symbol to bolster their own sense of racial and regional pride. Daniel drives his truck around town, urging young Black teens to adopt the Confederate flag as their own, which they do, until "many cars and trucks in Columbus, South Carolina, sporting Confederate flags [were] being driven by black people."

But the real coup is when Daniel plays "Dixieland" at a Black medical association banquet. The doctors, taken aback, begin laughing, and from there the rebel flag becomes adopted by "black businessmen and ministers" and by "a black land grant institution in Orangeburg." The flag is flown at Black family reunions and picnics, until it is finally and "quietly dismissed from its station with the U.S. and state flags atop the State Capitol."

Written years before the shooting in the Emanuel African Methodist Episcopal Church which initiated the South Carolina state legislature's 2015 decision to take down the Confederate flag, Everett's story is a blend of social realism, satire, and allegory. You might see Daniel's appropriation of the Confederate flag and "Dixieland" as analogous to the appropriation of the n-word by African Americans. Or perhaps you might see the story as the silver lining to one popular argument against appropriation, which is that it renders invisible the culture from which material objects or aesthetics have been taken. But in Everett's story, everyone appropriates. Poor Whites appropriate culture, poor Blacks appropriate culture, wealthy Blacks appropriate culture. African Americans can appropriate White cultural narratives and, by doing so, erase the power, the meaning, and even the existence of those symbols. Invisibility, in this sense, is not the unfortunate by-product of appropriation, but the goal.

That said, the fact that Daniel's race comes to light only after a studied examination of his class highlights the role money plays in cultural appropriation and ownership. Appropriation is not just the casual work of teens: it has to be done by doctors, businesspeople, lawyers and ministers. An entire middle-class culture has to engage in it. Everett's focus on money is also, oddly, one of the reasons Travis and Barb don't come off as monsters, since the White couple's racism is contextualized by their poverty. During their interaction, Daniel holds all the power because he can afford to buy the truck; he also subtly, but pointedly, humiliates Travis by offering him more for the truck than Travis wanted to charge, just to make Travis act as Daniel's delivery boy.

Many of us might not agree with Daniel that White and Black Southern culture are so inextricably bound. You might cringe in fear when he addresses as "brothers" a group of White men who threaten to beat him up over his use of the Confederate flag. But Everett's story makes a convincing case that these different groups are, by their shared history of slavery and violence, war and money, brothers. The complex ways in which all the characters in this story appropriate one another's symbols and cultural artifacts awaken the reader to a larger sense of who gets erased from American history, but how the culturally invisible might, figuratively and literally, buy their way back in. In Everett's story, racist symbols are not static metaphors of racial inferiority or dominance. Instead, they become adaptive carriers of historical meaning. They can be owned by anyone.

In that, "Appropriation of Cultures" reminds me of my earlier argument about *The Iliad*, and the possibility that, over time, nearly all texts can be de-authored and de-cultured. Is de-culturing finally a positive or negative process, or a little of both? Adapted and appropriated texts, by being internationally shared and reimagined, of course lose the sheen of their cultural authenticity. Their appropriation means I lose the particular sense of their history, place, and the community that originally authored them. But doesn't the long span of human history mean I was always going to lose these things? By losing cultural specificity, perhaps I gain a larger, more globally shared sense of authorship. I learn that power is not always and only located in the same centers, but may be shared or taken, as formerly dispossessed communities rewrite the majority's narratives. I see this in Kehinde Wiley's elaborate and jewel-toned portraits, in which he paints young African American and Nigerian subjects in poses they themselves select from Old World portraits of European royalty. These portraits

rely on motif appropriation to reframe my ideas of Western portrai-
ture, centering Black men at the heart, not the margins, of Western
power. By adapting these iconic paintings for his own use, Wiley shows
me that the Western art tradition can belong to anyone who wishes to
claim it. Wiley's motif appropriation does not rely upon the notion
that we are all at heart and in body the same; instead, it suggests that
we might become equal partners in the creation, dissemination, and
even ownership of the same cultural narratives around power.

Appropriation might even bring other marginalized communities together through art forms and products that represent themes of
social resistance. Hip-hop, for example, which has its roots in post–
Civil Rights era South Bronx, is now written and performed by politically underrepresented groups throughout the world, such as Malawi
teens in Nkhata Bay critiquing a repressive regime, or Turks fighting
for civil rights, or Cuban youths arguing for political equality. The cultural authenticity of African American hip-hop has been transformed
by other marginalized groups across the globe, who see American hip-
hop as a direct and original expression of their own ethnic struggles.

I was thinking about American hip-hop recently after watching
a short video on the *New York Times* website about Japan's fascination with Chicano subculture. The interviewer, a young Chicano
man from L.A., spoke with a variety of lowrider car enthusiasts, rap-
pers, and Chicano-style clothing-store owners with respect but also
some skepticism. The Japanese appropriation of Chicano culture is,
of course, in part about money—importing and selling clothes, cars,
music, and identities. But for some Japanese, it has also become a
kind of radical self-recognition. One young woman, a rapper named
MoNa a.k.a. Sad Girl, in fact felt as if some unspoken aspect of her
Japanese family dynamic was best expressed and resolved in the lan-

guage of Chicano-style rap. It was *because* of learning about Chicano culture, she said, that she learned how to respect her own family. In her words, she was "saved because of this culture." Critics might find these statements naïve or self-serving, but does that matter? It strikes me that if we dismiss appropriation as solely a colonial practice or the reification of stereotypes about others, we miss how appropriation may reinforce positive values and clarify aesthetics we already hold *within ourselves*. Appropriation may be less a process of taking, then, than one of revealing another dimension to our identities.

APPROPRIATION AS SURVIVAL

In my last letter to you, I spoke about writers who fake racial identities on the page, but there are writers—and people—who, like MoNa a.k.a. Sad Girl, fake or appropriate identities off the page as well. To me, this extends far beyond the problem of trying to capitalize upon the cultural identities of other people in order to publish or disseminate your own work; perhaps it's not about publication at all. I say this because as I write you now, the story of one such writer has come to light. His name is Hermán G. Carrillo—"Hache" to his friends—and before his death from Covid-19 and the publication of his *Washington Post* obituary, he lived life as a creative writing professor and Cuban immigrant who, as a child in 1967, fled Castro-led Cuba with his parents. Arriving in the United States after stints in Spain and Florida, Carrillo's family purportedly settled in Michigan, where the young Carrillo became a piano prodigy. After losing interest in piano, however, Carrillo turned to writing, and, in 2004, published his first and only novel, *Loosing My Espanish*, which depicts the story of a Chicago teacher who tries, and fails, to inspire an interest in history in his U.S.-bred Cuban American students.

"Hache" Carrillo was a beloved teacher at George Washington University, an acclaimed novelist, a gardening enthusiast, and chairman of the literary PEN/Faulkner Foundation. He was also Herman Glenn Carroll, an African American man born and raised in Michigan, whose family has been confounded and hurt by his fake identity, and whose own husband only learned of his actual biography after his death.

I never knew Carrillo myself, but I know people who did, and all of them are reeling from the revelation. Many on social media have howled with outrage, but Carrillo's friends defend him, as much out of love for their memory of "Hache" as out of sympathy for his husband. No one, not even Carrillo's family, it seems, can locate a reason for the deception, though many have latched on to something Carrillo's former mentor, the writer Helena María Viramontes, said in his obituary: Carrillo's stories, she told the reporter, "centered on lonely cultural misfits, striving and striving, in whatever crazy situations they were in, to find a sense of belonging."

What if there are performances of self that, if not biographically true, help a person become someone she always in essence wanted to be: perhaps a kinder spouse, a more attentive parent, a forgiving teacher? People like Rachel Dolezal, a White woman from a racist and physically abusive family who later reaped public scorn for trying to pass as Black: how much of her appropriation was an attempt to heal pain that couldn't be resolved within what she saw as the oppressive restraints of her race? Likely Carrillo did see in the identity of the Cuban immigrant a metaphor for some interior, psychic difference of self that he either felt he lacked or wanted to amplify.

Much could be speculated about, if never settled by, Carrillo's identity as a gay African American man growing up at a time when such an identity would be particularly fraught. What if his false identity strengthened some resolve he didn't believe he possessed, one that allowed for a different relationship with his community? What if he could be more authentically himself because of the lie?

But I wonder, too, if I'm sympathetic to Carrillo's appropriation because of my own identity, not just as a writer, but as a biracial woman who reads to many as White, whose insistence on her own biraciality has perhaps struck others—as it has sometimes struck me—as some particularly recalcitrant performance, something false and self-serving, so culturally vague as to be finally meaningless? There have been many times in my life when, looking into a mirror, I've wondered exactly who, and what, I am. Of course, I can prove some part of my identity via blood, but that's not a foundation to lay a personhood upon. Something about me, I tell myself, must be more substantial than DNA. What if this is what Carrillo was looking for, a selfhood that was inherently more stable, more nourishing than the one he'd been born into?

But there is a darker truth, too, to Carrillo's story and to writing, and that is the pull a good self-narrative can have on one's imagination, tugging you quietly into its orbit so that the more you relax your scruples, the faster you find yourself drifting into an alternate world of events, characters, and facts. Lillian Hellman was one such writer whose self-aggrandizement unmoored her from reality. Perhaps for some, the porousness between text and self is larger than most, and perhaps these writers like the attention their lies attract, reveling in the admiration and sympathies they garner, making them feel part of a world that would otherwise shut them out.

Clearly, none of this behavior is right. My sympathies aren't meant to rescue the lies, and I don't view the ethical lapses of Carrillo's novel in any different light than I do the poems of Araki Yasusada. But as with so many issues raised by appropriation, Carrillo's deception also seems to evade clear categories of right and wrong: how empathetically I react to his fake identity is based on how much I suspect the "right" psychological outcomes outweighed or even necessitated his wrong behavior. For many reasons, X, I would hope you don't take the path Carrillo did, not just because his deception was monumentally painful for those who loved him, but because it was also, I suspect, a performance he needed to survive.

Carrillo's story again highlights for me the most flummoxing paradox of appropriation: it is a private creative endeavor that both relies upon and then appears selfishly to dismiss the public weight of history. Perhaps it's a fantasist's desire, X, to think appropriation can help heal personal wounds, or neutralize the meanings of negative texts, symbols, or artifacts. Perhaps it's simplistic to argue that appropriation offers us a way to return humanity—and visibility—to the people whom racist symbols, objects, and institutions would erase. Returning for a moment to Everett's short story and the Confederate flag, perhaps we *shouldn't* want to appropriate all symbols, but fight instead to preserve certain objects' original authorship and context. Some artifacts, like the swastika, for example, may never and should never be neutralized through appropriation. We need to remember the specific meanings behind these symbols and texts *because* they are painful, and because without the reminder of these traumas vivid in our communal memories, we might downplay their real transgenerational effects.

I wrote before that appropriation can never stand in for the hard work of real-world activism. I stand by that, but I will add here that if you treat appropriation as a solely negative practice, you ignore one of its accidental benefits, which is that it enlarges, rather than shrinks, our sense of connection by requiring us to interrogate the historically enmeshed relationships we have, and don't have, with one another. Part of understanding how we are intertwined comes through the creation of art, which requires that we make ourselves and our art vulnerable to the gaze of others. Once our art has been seen, however, it can be shared, interpreted, and even translated for a new audience, one whose responses we can neither anticipate nor control. On the one hand, sharing art means that our own artistic practices and subjects might also be transformed without our consent. On the other, this allows for us to transmit our private lives and art forms to others, encouraging the expansion of smaller communal histories into a larger, collectively shared memory, one that might even allow people to reframe the writing of their own histories and identities in response. Is it worth risking your particular cultural claim to certain subjects in order for all writers to pursue the larger goal of art, which is to expand, rather than contract, historical memory? Or does historical memory require that only certain people can and must remember?

If you approach appropriation with any ethical seriousness, X, you will have to think deeply about aesthetics, history, and difference; you will reevaluate the literary and humanistic values you claim to hold, on the page and in the publishing industry, and you will have to consider the role that money and commercialism play in art. You will have to consider not only how writing has failed us but also how it's inspired social change. Literary language may have limited political effects in the short term, X, and it may, as I wrote you before, be easily manipulated, but in the long term, I think we can see that our depictions of women, people of color, and the disabled have changed dramatically. If we've become attuned to how politicians and writers use metaphor as ways to promote policies that have substantial negative effects, we've also used metaphor to contradict them. Our rejections of their appropriations have compelled us, generation by generation, to reimagine more nuanced and realistic language around bodily difference.

Perhaps, having read my letters, you'll decide there's no benefit to appropriation, and no possibility of respectfully appropriating either, so long as the literary system and the effects of colonialism remain in place. And so to enable more creative freedom for everyone, perhaps you'll argue that the establishment really should be torn down, in the hopes that dismantling the structure will allow for a better, sturdier replacement. But dismantling the structure does not ensure or require that a better one will take its place, X. Something else will rise, and I suspect it will more or less resemble what came before in its entrenched codes of hierarchy, capital, prestige, and control. The bodies at the head of this new structure may look different, but the effects will likely be the same.

That may be pessimistic, but my cynicism about academia or the literary industry doesn't diminish the great pleasure I get from writing, reading, and teaching. And that's the final thing I want to tell you about appropriation, X, which is that the creative life is profoundly fun. I write in order to lose myself in images and stories I can't consciously force myself to envision, and part of the pleasure in losing myself is risk: the risk of getting something wrong, or—when it comes to memoir—maybe getting something too unpleasantly right; the risk of not knowing what I'm saying or where I'm headed; the risk of not knowing who my poems' speakers are, maybe not even knowing who I am as an author. Writing has surprised me into insights I couldn't have articulated except through intense creative play. Lionel Shriver is right: Reading a story or a poem in which the author goes so far past what we expect or believe she could achieve is thrilling, not unlike watching someone compete at the very highest level of the Olympics. Can she do it? Can she really pull that off? If she can, fantastic. If she can't, well, why despise her for trying?

So. These are some of my thoughts about appropriation. You can decide to pursue this practice or not in your art, but your choice will never automatically sanction or damn you. I believe you want to be respectful and also innovative, and I want to remind you that, when it comes to appropriation, one virtue does not require the sacrifice of another. It does mean, however, that regardless of your choice, your decision should arise from becoming the most compassionate and inquisitive person that you can. You alone will decide how to act and what to publish, if not always what to write. Your identity as a writer will be shaped by your experience in the world; by how our definitions of culture and race change; by how literary communities rise up, coalesce, and maybe even fall around you. Over the course of your life, you will be many different people, and many different writers, not all of whom you'll admire. You will surprise yourself into empathetic insights through your work, and you will, unconsciously, reflect and refract the prejudices that shaped you. And if you are very, very lucky, X, you will be able to write and publish for the rest of your life.

My father, when I was a teenager, used to usher me out the door each day by singing out, "Go forth, and do good works!" He meant it as a joke, because he knew I hated the Catholic school I attended, but in the end, I think my father's words are right. Go forth and do good works, X.

It's all that we can do in life.

Some Questions to Consider
A Postscript

While no specific student exists to whom I wrote this series of letters—because that would be not only appropriative but a FERPA violation—this book evolved from a series of conversations and encounters I've had with students and colleagues over the years. With their help, I've drafted some questions you might bring into class to help frame your own conversation around creative work that engages in subject or motif appropriation. None of these questions should, if considered honestly by the writer, generate easy answers or produce automatically unassailable results; there may not even be consistently "good" answers to these questions, as texts can do both sophisticated and regressive things at once. Instead these questions should help writers reevaluate the spirit and intent of their project, to clarify both their depictions of the identities on the page and perhaps their creative resolve. I hope these questions help young writers identify for themselves the ways in which cultural approximations might—and might not—verge into cultural appropriation.

- What are the metaphors—conscious or inadvertent— that you have created around racial meaning in your project?
- Have you seen these particular metaphors before in other works of literature or art and, if so, in what ways do your own metaphors replicate or disrupt hierarchies you are already familiar with?
- Is your understanding of your own identity at the margin or the center of the story? Are your characters reflections of you right now, or reflections of how you might behave in specific circumstances and conditions?
- What kinds and types of interactions have you had with the communities you wish to represent?
- In what small and large ways have those interactions informed your research, your perception of your characters, and your writing?
- Which books, films, and art have you studied by the identities you wish to represent? Which ones are most relevant to your project?
- In what ways have you translated your research into character behaviors, speech patterns, insights, and self-perceptions that reveal how the character's self-perception and activity in her fictional world are flexible, and based on her interaction with other people and social forces she does not control?

- Understanding that some may see any act of literary appropriation as the continuing practice of colonialism, what value and message do you see attached to your creative project?
- What are the reasons your particular project needs to be written and published by you? What desires do you hold about either your characters or your project?
- Which audience is your project ultimately suited for, and how does your text signal that?

Feel free to add other questions to this list based on issues raised by this book, or by your students' concerns.

Acknowledgments

So many conversations with fellow writers, poets, teachers, editors, and students helped me with this project. Thank you to Scott Black and Sarita Gaytan. Thank you to Rick Barot, Jericho Brown, Geffrey Davis, and Marie Mockett for the asides, the anecdotes, the observations, the important questions. Thank you to my students, especially those who endured past workshops with me in which this very topic sparked anger, confusion, or pain, with few cogent results. I owe you; this book is my offering. Thank you to my father, with whom I'm always arguing. Thank you to Jill Bialosky and Drew Weitman for their excellent suggestions and editorial eyes. Thank you, as always, to Sean Myles, who walked the dog and got takeout so I could work and, during lockdown, ate what hadn't rotted in our refrigerator without complaint. Thank you to my colleagues at the University of Utah. And thank you—finally, eternally—to Melanie

Rae Thon for the multiple close reads, and the belief that making literature is a spiritual endeavor. You make me rethink the very practice and purpose of writing. I thank you for your heart, your mind, your friendship: I thank you for your presence in my life.

Notes

LETTER ONE: AN INVITATION

6   "Climbing the stairway": William Meredith, "Effort at Speech," in *Effort at Speech: New and Selected Poems* (Chicago: TriQuarterly Books, 1997), 100–1.

10 violence that had only amplified during the early 1980s: Ibram X. Kendi, *How to Be an Antiracist* (New York: One World, 2019), 27.

LETTER TWO: SETTING THE TERMS

19 As the scholar Pascal Nicklas notes in his book: Pascal Nicklas, *Adaptation and Cultural Appropriation: Literature, Film, and the Arts* (Berlin: DeGruyter, 2012), 6.

20 The critic Julie Sanders, in her book: Julie Sanders, *Adaptation and Appropriation* (New York: Routledge, 2005), 1.

21 "a more decisive journey": Sanders, *Adaptation and Appropriation,* 1.

21 Adaptation, in this sense, shades uncomfortably into plagiarism: "Code of Best Practices in Fair Use for Poetry," eds. Patricia Aufderheide, Katharine Coles, Peter Jaszi, Jennifer Urban (American University School of Communication's Center for Social Media, 2011), 8. Online January 2011,

accessed November 22, 2019, http://archive.cmsimpact.org/sites/default/files/documents/pages/fairusepoetrybooklet_singlepg_3.pdf.

23 The philosopher James O. Young, in his book: James O. Young, *Cultural Appropriation and the Arts* (Malden, MA: Blackwell Publishing, 2008), 6.

23 In it, Shriver declared: Lionel Shriver, "Lionel Shriver's Full Speech: 'I Hope the Concept of Cultural Appropriation Is a Passing Fad,'" *The Guardian*, September 13, 2016, accessed November 22, 2019, https://www.theguardian.com/commentisfree/2016/sep/13/lionel-shrivers-full-speech-i-hope-the-concept-of-cultural-appropriation-is-a-passing-fad.

24 Shriver's argument duplicates: Margaret Drabble, *The Red Queen: A Transcultural Tragicomedy* (Orlando: Harcourt, 2004), 9.

24 later walked these comments back: Annasue McCleave Wilson, "Manners Matter in Writing: Margaret Drabble," *Publishers Weekly Online*, February 10, 2017, accessed November 22, 2019, https://www.publishersweekly.com/pw/by-topic/authors/profiles/article/72758-manners-matter-in-writing-margaret-drabble.html.

24 Shriver amplified her argument: Debbie Zhou, "Lionel Shriver Returns to Australia and Doubles Down on 'Fascistic' Identity Politics," *The Guardian*, September 1, 2019, accessed November 22, 2019, https://www.theguardian.com/books/2019/sep/02/lionel-shriver-returns-to-australia-and-doubles-down-on-fascistic-identity-politics.

25 "intellectual property, traditional knowledge": Susan Scafidi, *Who Owns Culture? Appropriation and Authenticity in American Law* (New Brunswick: Rutgers University Press, 2005), 26.

27 violated the international boycott: Jordan Runtagh, "Paul Simon's 'Graceland': 10 Things You Didn't Know," *Rolling Stone*, August 25, 2016, accessed March 5, 2020, https://www.rollingstone.com/music/music-features/paul-simons-graceland-10-things-you-didnt-know-105220/.

28 "Homer" is a series of poets: Homer, *The Odyssey*, trans. Emily Wilson (New York: W. W. Norton, 2018), 10–12.

30 "a way of coming to terms": Edward Said, *Orientalism* (New York: Pantheon Books, 1978), 1–3.

32 found it adorable: Sean Rossman, "Chinese Are OK with Utah Teen's Controversial Cheongsam Prom Dress," *USA Today*, May 4, 2018, accessed November 22, 2019, https://www.usatoday.com/story/news/nation-now/2018/05/04/chinese-ok-utah-teens-controversial-cheongsam-prom-dress/580062002/.

33 Pharrell Williams wearing a warrior bonnet: *Elle UK*, cover, July 2014.

37 the conceptual poet and artist Kenneth Goldsmith: Alec Wilkinson, "Something Borrowed," *The New Yorker*, October 2, 2015.

39 "felt like a five year-old holding Hulk Hogan": Lauren Williams, "The Terrifying Racial Stereotypes Laced Through Darren Wilson's Testimony," *Vox*, November 25, 2014, Accessed November 22, 2019, https://www.vox.com/2014/11/25/7283327/michael-brown-racist-stereotypes.

41 "of referring to and disguising forces": Toni Morrison, *Playing in the Dark: Whiteness and the Literary Imagination* (Cambridge: Harvard University Press, 1992), 63.

46 Carl Linnaeus created human racial hierarchies: Kendi, *How to Be an Antiracist*, 41.

46 "a trope of ultimate, irreducible difference": Henry Louis Gates Jr., *The Henry Louis Gates, Jr. Reader*, ed. Abby Wolf (Boston: Basic Books, 2012), 216.

46 a careless use of language: Gates Jr., *The Henry Louis Gates, Jr. Reader*, 225.

46 Katy Perry, dressed as a geisha: Posted by Juan Pablo, YouTube, uploaded November 24, 2013, and accessed November 22, 2019, https://www.youtube.com/watch?v=iXqcjgX-I9E.

49 "the peculiar social, cultural, economic": LeRoi Jones [Amiri Baraka], *Blues People* (New York: William Morrow, 1963), 151, 154.

50 "the boundaries of one's imaginative sympathy": *The Racial Imaginary: Writers on Race in the Life of the Mind*, eds., Beth Loffreda and Claudia Rankine (New York: Fence Books, 2015), 17.

51 "[C]an I write from another's point of view": Loffreda and Rankine, *The Racial Imaginary*, 17–18.

52 "Empathy" is a word that shows up: Alison Landsberg, *Prosthetic Memory: The Transformation of American Remembrance in the Age of Mass Culture* (New York: Columbia University Press, 2004), 170.

54 Hannah Arendt's theory of "representative thinking": Namwali Serpell, "The Banality of Empathy," *The New York Review of Books*, March 2, 2019, accessed November 22, 2019, https://www.nybooks.com/daily/2019/03/02/the-banality-of-empathy/.

LETTER THREE: TRUTH, ACCURACY, AND
THE COMMODIFICATION OF IDENTITY

58 "If you got hiv": Anders Carlson-Wee, "How-To," *The Nation*, July 30-August 6, 2018, accessed November 22, 2019, https://www.thenation.com/article/how-to/.

61   The playwright and actress Anna Deavere Smith: Anna Deavere Smith, *Fires in the Mirror* (New York: Anchor, 1993), xxiv.

66   "I [began] to possess her without tenderness": William Styron, *The Confessions of Nat Turner* (New York: Random House, 1967), 264.

66   "glimpse of the dim shadowed cleft": Styron, *Nat Turner*, 338.

66   "[H]ad I not been a Negro": Styron, *Nat Turner*, 322, 339.

66   "spend[ing] upon [Margaret] all afternoon": Styron, *Nat Turner*, 354.

67   "[s]lumbrous in broad daylight": Styron, *Nat Turner*, 224.

68   Meanwhile, Turner's imagined celibacy: John McMillian, "The Politics of Identity in an Era of 'Nation Building': William Styron's 'The Confessions of Nat Turner,'" *The Centennial Review* 41, no. 3 (1997), 485.

68   "an eighteen-year-old nubile": Donald W. Markos, "Margaret Whitehead in 'The Confessions of Nat Turner,'" *Studies in the Novel* 4, no. 1 (1972), 53.

69   "I hear tell a nigger boy's" Styron, *Nat Turner*, 237.

69   Published in 1967 during the rising "Black Power": McMillian "Politics of Identity," 479.

72   "wished someone slightly browner": Jeanine Cummins, *American Dirt*, Flatiron Books, 2020, 382.

72   noting also in an interview on NPR's *Latino USA*: Antonia Cereijido, "Digging into 'American Dirt,'" *Latino USA*, January 29, 2020, accessed March 5, 2020, https://www.latinousa.org/2020/01/29/americandirt/.

73   "[t]oday is Saturday, April 7, his cousin": Cummins, *American Dirt,* 4.

73   "[T]wo dozen law enforcement and medical personnel mov[e]": Cummins, *American Dirt*, 9.

74   "bodies that are no longer bodies": Cummins, *American Dirt*, 11.

75   "Luca . . . starts to understand": Cummins, *American Dirt,* 166.

75   "After a young, beautiful teen": Cummins, American Dirt, 252.

76   "despite everything they've suffered": Cummins, American Dirt, 373.

76   "as other critics have suggested": Jess Row, "American Dirt and the Tradition of the Moral Parable," *Los Angeles Times*, January 30, 2020, accessed September 20, 2020, https://www.latimes.com/entertainment-arts/books/story/2020-01-30/jess-row-on-sentimental-art-including-jeanine-cummins.

76   "dishonesty, [its] inability to feel": James Baldwin, "Everybody's Protest Novel," *Notes of a Native Son*, Beacon Press, 1955, 14, 21.

80   "reduce the blind spots": Lisa Halliday, *Asymmetry* (New York: Simon & Schuster, 2018), 216.

81   "be a bridge" and "telling this story": Cummins, *American Dirt*, 382.

82   Sandra Cisneros, who blurbed *American Dirt* positively: Cereijido, "Digging into 'American Dirt.'"

82   "Trojan Horse": Cereijido, "Digging into 'American Dirt.'"

82   2020 viral hashtag #PublishingPaidMe: Concepción de León and Elizabeth A. Harris, "#PublishingPaidMe and a Day of Action Reveal an Industry Reckoning," *The New York Times*, June 8, 2020, accessed June 10, 2020, https://www.nytimes.com/2020/06/08/books/publishingpaidme-publishing-day-of-action.html

82   Stanford University Literary Lab: Laura B. McGrath, "Comping White," *Los Angeles Review of Books*, January 21, 2019, accessed June 5, 2020, https://lareviewofbooks.org/article/comping-white/.

86   Thus you understand that a historic: Henry Louis Gates Jr., *The Henry Louis Gates, Jr. Reader*, ed. Abby Wolf (Boston: Basic Books, 2012), 219.

87   "acknowledge the massively knotted . . . histories,": Said, *Orientalism*, 31.

89   as the critic Jess Row noted: Jess Row, "*American Dirt* and the Tradition of the Moral Parable," Los Angeles Times, January 30, 2020, accessed September 20, 2020, https://www.latimes.com/entertainment-arts/books/story/2020-01-30/jess-row-on-sentimental-art-including-jeanine-cummins.

89   *The Turner Diaries* . . . with its depiction of a race war: Camille Jackson, "The Turner Diaries, Other Racist Novels, Inspire Extremist Violence," The Southern Poverty Law Center, October 14, 2004, accessed March 5, 2020, https://www.splcenter.org/fighting-hate/intelligence-report/2004/turner-diaries-other-racist-novels-inspire-extremist-violence.

90   "is not, after all, merely": Baldwin, *Notes of a Native Son*, 15.

LETTER FOUR: IDENTITY AS ENCOUNTER

93   "certain inward sense": William Styron, *The Confessions of Nat Turner* (New York: Random House, 1967), 53.

93   This is something W.E.B. Du Bois asked: W.E.B. Du Bois, *The Souls of Black Folk* (CreateSpace Independent Publishing Platform, 2014), 52, 45.

94   "Helen is telling the colonel about the ship now": Peter Ho Davies, "The Hull Case," *Equal Love* (New York: Houghton Mifflin, 2000), 1.

95   "Henry thought the lights were a cop at first": Davies, *Equal Love*, 2.

96   "They kn[ew] better than to try": Davies, *Equal Love*, 3.

98   Nick's father, a doctor, helps: Ernest Hemingway, "Indian Camp," in *The Complete Short Stories of Ernest Hemingway* (New York: Scribner, 1987), 67–70.

99   Disdain is the presiding emotion: David Treuer, lecture on cultural

appropriation at Bread Loaf Writers Conference, 2018, accessed November 22, 2019, https://midd.hosted.panopto.com/Panopto/Pages/Viewer .aspx?id=9a59c577–37cc–4d73–8ea4–a94400ffe540.

101   "Into the shadow": *The Ella Higginson Blog*, accessed November 22, 2019, https://ellahigginson.blogspot.com/p/the-vanishing-race.html.

105   "the worst racists in the world": Maureen F. McHugh, *China Mountain Zhang* (New York: Tom Doherty Associates, 1992), 61.

106   "free when [he] slip[s] between the cracks": McHugh, *China Mountain Zhang*, 60.

108   "suggest one racial group is superior": Ibram X. Kendi, *How to Be an Antiracist* (New York: One World, 2019), 20.

109   "We, whose shame, humiliation": W.E.B. Du Bois, "The Souls of White Folk," in *W.E.B. Du Bois: A Reader*, ed. David Levering Lewis (New York: Holt, 1995), 456.

110   Patricia Smith's 1992 persona poem: Patricia Smith, "Skinhead," *AGNI Online*, posted October 15, 1992, and accessed November 22, 2019, https:// agnionline.bu.edu/poetry/skinhead.

113   "On the day the sienna-skinned man": Ai, "Killing Floor," in *Vice: New and Selected Poems* (New York: W. W. Norton, 1979), 21–23.

116   "[we] strip away the tattered fabric": Ai, "Testimony of J. Robert Oppenheimer," in *Vice*, 77–79.

117   "a spy, a sleeper, a spook": Viet Thanh Nguyen, *The Sympathizer* (New York: Grove Press, 2016), 1.

118   "When your baby dies it's never an accident": Chang Rae Lee, *Native Speaker* (New York: Riverhead, 1996), 129.

LETTER FIVE: APPROPRIATION AS RACIAL HOAX

124   In 2015, *The Best American Poetry* series: Isaac Fitzgerald, "White Writer Makes 'Best Poetry'—With an Asian Pen Name," *Buzzfeed News*, September 7, 2015, accessed November 22, 2019, https://www.buzzfeednews.com/ article/isaacfitzgerald/yi-fen-chou-is-michael-derrick-hudson.

128   "Only in America could it occur": Charles Yu, "In America," in *Quiet Fire: Asian American Poetry, 1892–1970*, ed. Juliana Chang (PA: Temple University Press, 1998), 59.

131   "Am I supposed to say something": Yi-Fen Chou, "The Bees, the Flowers, Jesus, Ancient Tigers, Poseidon, Adam and Eve," in *The Best American Poetry 2015*, eds. Sherman Alexie and David Lehman (New York: Scribner, 2015), 25–26.

131   a theory proven by the fact he once appeared: William Targ, *Indecent Plea-sures: The Life and Colorful Times of William Targ* (New York: Macmillan, 1975), 59.

132   Yasusada simply refers to as "they": Araki Yasusada, "Walkers with Ladle," in *Doubled Flowering: From the Notebooks of Araki Yasusada* (New York: Roof Books, 1997), 30.

134   "Walking in the vegetable patch": Araki Yasusada, "Mad Daughter and Big-Bang," in *Doubled Flowering*, 11.

135   "spread[ing] out like a cloud of sperm": Araki Yasusada, "Telescope with Urn," in *Doubled Flowering*, 32.

139   "all-consuming web of deceit": Christopher L. Miller, *Imposters: Literary Hoaxes and Cultural Authenticity* (Chicago: University of Chicago Press, 2018), 35.

140   Albert argued that she'd been sexually abused: Miller, *Imposters,* 37.

141   "We figured he was probably in prison": Louis Menand, "Literary Hoaxes and the Ethics of Authorship," *The New Yorker*, December 3, 2018, accessed November 22, 2019, https://www.newyorker.com/magazine/2018/12/10/literary-hoaxes-and-the-ethics-of-authorship.

142   Kevin Young, in his book *Bunk*: Kevin Young, "Moon Shot: Race, A Hoax, and the Birth of Fake News," *The New Yorker,* October 21, 2017, accessed November 22, 2019, https://www.newyorker.com/books/page-turner/moon-shot-race-a-hoax-and-the-birth-of-fake-news.

143   "Two daikons": Yasusada, [Untitled fragment], in *Doubled Flowering*, 26.

144   "American circus": Yasusada, [Untitled haiku], in *Doubled Flowering*, 43.

145   "Indeed, it has been the common assumption": Yasusada, "Appendix," *Doubled Flowering*, 124.

145   The literary critic Marjorie Perloff: Marjorie Perloff, "In Search of the Authentic Other: The Poetry of Araki Yasusada," *Electronic Poetry Center*, accessed March 5, 2020, http://writing.upenn.edu/epc/authors/perloff/boston.html.

145   "surely not unintention[al]": Perloff, "In Search of the Authentic Other."

LETTER SIX: APPROPRIATION AND REHABILITATION

164   Brian Morton, a novelist and professor: Brian Morton, "Virginia Woolf? Snob! Richard Wright? Sexist! Dostoevsky? Anti-Semite!" *The New York Times*, January 8, 2019, accessed November 22, 2019, https://www.nytimes.com/2019/01/08/books/review/edith-wharton-house-of-mirth-anti-semitism.html.

165   Letters to his father while Faulkner was a student: Philip Cohen, "Faulkner and Racism: A Commentary on Arthur F. Kinney's 'Faulkner and Racism,'" *Connotations* 5, no. 1 (1995–96), 108.

165   Compounding this depiction of the Strothers: William Faulkner, *Flags in the Dust* (New York: Vintage, 2012), 313–14.

166   Faulkner depicted Black characters: Cohen, "Faulkner and Racism," 110.

166   it was the same year he sent a letter: Cohen, "Faulkner and Racism," 108–9.

166   Thus the period in which Faulkner wrote: Cohen, "Faulkner and Racism," 117.

170   "The season turned": Tony Hoagland, "The Change," *Academy of American Poets*, 2003, accessed November 22, 2019, https://poets.org/poem/change.

173   a national confrontation: Claudia Rankine, "Open Letter: A Dialogue on Race and Poetry," *Academy of American Poets*, posted February 14, 2011, accessed November 22, 2019, https://poets.org/text/open-letter-dialogue -race-and-poetry. See Tony Hoagland's response, "Dear Claudia: A Letter in Response," *Academy of American Poets,* posted March 14, 2011, accessed November 22, 2019, https://poets.org/text/dear-claudia-letter-response.

179   "Daniel Barkley had money": Percival Everett, "Appropriation of Cultures," *Callaloo* 19, no. 1 (Winter, 1996), 24.

180   "He used the slide": Everett, "Appropriation of Cultures," 24–25.

181   "Barb sighed and asked": Everett, "Appropriation of Cultures," 28.

183   "quietly dismissed from its station": Everett, "Appropriation of Cultures," 30.

185   Hip-hop, for example: Evan Young, "'Keepin' It Real': Hip-Hop and Cultural Appropriation," *Medium*, posted April 18, 2016, accessed November 22, 2019, https://medium.com/@evanyoung/keepin-it-real-hip-hop-and -cultural-appropriation-ca3110cf64da.

185   Japan's fascination with Chicano subculture: Emily Rhine, Walter Thompson-Hernández, and Alexandra Eaton, "Inside Japan's Chicano Subculture," *The New York Times*, posted February 19, 2019, accessed March 15, 2020, https://www.nytimes.com/video/style/100000005806771/japan -chicano-culture.html?action=click&gtype=vhs&version=vhs-heading&m odule=vhs&region=title-area&cview=true&t=401.

186   His name is Hermán G. Carrillo: Paul Duggan, "Novelist H. G. Carrillo, Who Explored Themes of Cultural Alienation, Dies After Developing Covid-19," *The Washington Post*, posted May 23, 2020, accessed June 1, 2020, https:// www.washingtonpost.com/local/cuban-american-author-hg-carrillo-who -explored-themes-of-cultural-alienation-died-after-contracting-covid -19/2020/05/21/35478894-97d8-11ea-91d7-cf4423d47683_story.html.

187   "centered on lonely": Duggan, "Novelist H. G. Carrillo."

Suggested Further Reading

Appiah, Kwame Anthony. *The Ethics of Identity*. Princeton: Princeton University Press, 2005.

——. *The Reith Lectures*. BBC Radio 4, https://www.bbc.co.uk/programmes/articles/2sM4D6LTTVlFZhbMpmfYmx6/kwame-anthony-appiah.

Du Bois, W.E.B. "The Souls of Black Folks." In *The W.E.B. Du Bois Reader*. Edited by David Levering Lewis. New York: Holt, 1995.

Clift, Robert, dir. *Blacking Up: Hip-Hop's Remix of Race and Identity*. California Newsreel, 2011.

Currie, Gregory. "The Authentic and the Aesthetic." *American Philosophical Quarterly* 22 (1985): 153–60.

Gates, Henry Louis Jr. " 'Authenticity,' or the Lesson of Little Tree." *New York Times Book Review*, November 24, 1991.

Kendi, Ibram X. *How to Be an Antiracist*. New York: One World, 2019.

Loffreda, Beth, and Claudia Rankine, eds. *The Racial Imaginary: Writers on Race in the Life of the Mind*. New York: Fence Books, 2015.

Miller, Christopher L. *Imposters: Literary Hoaxes and Cultural Authenticity*. Chicago: University of Chicago Press, 2018.

Morrison, Toni. *Playing in the Dark: Whiteness and the Literary Imagination*. Cambridge: Harvard University Press, 1992.

Said, Edward. *Orientalism*. New York: Pantheon Books, 1978.

Scafidi, Susan. *Who Owns Culture? Appropriation and Authenticity in American Law*. New Brunswick: Rutgers University Press, 2005.

Serpell, Namwali. "The Banality of Empathy." *New York Review of Books*, March 2, 2019.

Smith, Zadie. "Fascinated to Presume: In Defense of Fiction." *New York Review of Books*, October 24, 2019.

Taylor, Charles. *Multiculturalism: Examining the Politics of Recognition*. Princeton: Princeton University Press, 1994 revised edition.

Treuer, David. "Writing Culture: Some Thoughts on Difference, Appropriation, Politics, and Race in Modern Writing." 2018 Bread Loaf Lectures, https://midd.hosted.panopto.com/Panopto/Pages/Viewer.aspx?id=9a59c577–37cc-4d73–8ea4-a94400ffe540.

Young, James O. *Cultural Appropriation and the Arts*. Malden, MA: Blackwell Publishing, 2008.

Permissions

Index